Wonder Beasts

Wonder Beasts

Tales and Lore of the Phoenix, the Griffin, the Unicorn, and the Dragon

Joe Nigg

Libraries Unlimited, Inc.
Englewood, Colorado

1995

For
The J's of Phoenix, Arizona:
Joey, Jill, Jessie, Jayce,
and in memory of Julie

LIBRARIES UNLIMITED, INC.
P.O. Box 6633
Englewood, CO 80155-6633
1-800-237-6124

Production Editor: Louisa M. Griffin
Copy Editor: Tama J. Serfoss
Proofreader: Eileen Bartlett
Interior Book Design: Judy Gay Matthews

Library of Congress Cataloging-in-Publication Data

Nigg, Joe
   Wonder beasts : tales and lore of the phoenix, the griffin, the unicorn, and the dragon / Joe Nigg.
    xxvi, 160 p. 19x26 cm
    Includes bibliographical references and index.
    ISBN 1-56308-242-X
    1. Phoenix (Mythical bird) 2. Griffins. 3. Unicorns.
4. Dragons. I. Title.
GR830.P4N54 1995
398.24'54--dc20
                                          94-46797
                                            CIP

The Letter of
Prester John

In our land is a bird which is called Phenix. It is the fairest bird in all the world and there is no more than one in all the course of nature. He lives 100 years and then flies so high that the sun sets his wings afire. And then he comes down again to his nest, and there he burns to powder, and from the ashes comes a worm, and within 100 days after, there grows out of it another bird as fair as ever that other was.

* * *

Also in our land are gryffons. It is a great bird and a mighty, for he will carry to his nest an ox or a horse for his young birds to eat. In a town called Grounzwyk, in Saxony, is one of its claws which is as great as the horn of an ox.

* * *

And in our land are also unicorns. They are black and green and they slay many lions. And the lion slays the unicorn with subtleness. When the unicorn is resting at a tree, the lion comes and runs around the tree. The unicorn then runs after him and would fain slay him. Then he runs into the tree with his horn so hard that he cannot pull it out again. Then the lion comes and has mastery of the unicorn.

* * *

Also in our land is a tree that precious oil runs out of. There is a great serpent which that tree has in keeping all the whole year night and day. Only on St. John's day or night does the serpent or dragon sleep, and then we go to the tree and take that oil, which is no more than three pounds, and then we turn again with great dread and fear that he will see us and slay us. This tree is a day's journey from the paradise of the earth. But when this serpent is awakened, he moans loudly out of sorrow. This dragon has nine heads and two wings and is as big as two horses.

Fourteenth Century

Contents

The Phoenix

The Griffin

The Unicorn

The Dragon

Preface

Imaginary animals emerged from the mists of myth and oral tradition and for thousands of years were generally accepted as real animals in art and story. From one age to another, they took on different shapes and characters, reflecting major shifts of thought—even to the point of being discredited by seventeenth-century science. Immortal shapes, these mythical creatures survived in folklore and in heraldry and reappeared in nineteenth-century scholarship and children's literature. They are still with us, in scholarly works and fantasy fiction, in museums and movie theaters, heraldry and commercial packaging.

This collection introduces students to the history of wonder beasts through the rich, varied incarnations of the phoenix, griffin, unicorn, and dragon. These major figures still survive as images scattered throughout contemporary Western culture, and three of the four—the dragon, phoenix, and the unicorn—are among the four celestial animals of China. Their long histories and widespread presence make them preeminent among animals of the imagination. To follow their shifting literary shapes from their beginnings up to the present time is to catch glimpses of myth, religion, art, literature, and science through the ages.

Like most of the animals it deals with, *Wonder Beasts* is a hybrid. A combination of tales and lore, the collection presents primary sources within a context of background material. While the stories—told in a variety of literary styles—can certainly be enjoyed independently, the combination of entries and editorial text offers the reader fuller profiles of the animals than either could do separately. The introduction places the four major figures within the larger world of wonder beasts, and many of their relatives join them along the way. "The World of Ancient Beasts" map in the introduction and a bibliography and index in the back matter frame the diverse material. Traditional illustrations supplement the text.

Complete entries were selected whenever possible; those that were not self-contained are excerpted from longer works. Most titles of the latter pieces were composed by the editor. For authenticity, I retained variant translated spellings of the beasts' names, but modernized the spelling in archaic entries from Prester John and Edward Topsell. In modern translations and other entries, original British spelling is retained. I reformatted "The Phoenixes Are Flying" from its nineteenth-century prose translation, and broke into paragraphs long narrative sequences of "The Old Griffin" by the Brothers Grimm. Also, I retold "The Student and the Dragon King" from traditional sources and adapted "The Lambton Worm" from William Henderson's *Folklore of the Northern Counties of England and the Borders* (1866) and other traditional sources.

To encompass the multiple facets of the four major beasts, the material on each animal is divided into sections. An introduction to each beast presents the general image and characteristics of that creature.

"The [Phoenix, etc.] from the Past" surveys the traditional Western history of each animal, tracing the beast's changing roles through classical histories, medieval encyclopedias and bestiaries, travelers' tales, and Renaissance natural histories. The passages by such writers as Herodotus, Ctesias, and Pliny were regarded as authoritative and were repeated with variations by writer after writer up to the 1600s. This section usually ends with the scholarly debate over the animal's existence and the rejection of the creature as a real animal.

"The [Phoenix, etc.] Around the World" overlaps the preceding section in that it may also include ancient material. The emphasis here, though, is on the diversity of stories about the beast from around the world, and the different views of non-Western cultures toward the beast. This section gives the editor the opportunity to present many of the animal's fabulous relatives. Entries are primarily folktales in which the animal appears. *Folktale* is the more generic of the two terms; *fairy tale* is used primarily to emphasize magical and romantic elements.

When possible, I've selected tales in which the animal is a major figure; in other pieces, it is a secondary character responsible for initiating the plot or for moving the action forward. The animal is no longer one whose existence is seriously debated by scholars; here it is a shape of the imagination. In some of these stories, it is clearly the traditional creature, with its standard attributes. Sometimes it is derived from traditional images but is altered to fit local storytelling patterns, and in still other cases, the creature is an archetypal figure made individual by a given community. Of the four major wonder beasts, the dragon is the most universal, emerging seemingly independently in the tales of different ethnic groups, changing form from one society to another.

"The [Phoenix, etc.] Today" summarizes the beast's status since its nineteenth-century reappearance in books. Mythologists began analyzing the symbolic meanings of fabulous beasts and some post-Darwinian writers contended the animals existed before the great Flood. Most of the entries in this section represent the animals' new roles in modern children's literature and fantasy.

"More Wonder Beasts" contains many animals not dealt with previously in this book. The two excerpted entries—one ancient and the other from our own time—provide a yardstick by which to measure the transformation the animals have undergone in the period between an ancient natural history and a modern children's book.

The references section supplements the copyrighted sources listed in the acknowledgments and the sources cited for public domain entries.

While the commercial popularity of dragons and unicorns has been fairly recent, a substantial body of books dealing with fabulous beasts has been produced during the twentieth century. Major ones are cited in the bibliography. Among the many notable books for younger readers are Georgess McHargue's comprehensive *Beasts of Never* (1968) and Barbara Silverberg's standard *Phoenix Feathers: A Collection of Mythical Monsters* (1973). There are also collections of more contemporary material devoted only to dragons and unicorns.

I extend special thanks to the following for their valuable contributions to this book: David Loertscher, Vice President, Libraries Unlimited, for his initial interest in this subject and his editorial direction in its approach and arrangement; the Libraries Unlimited staff, notably editor Louisa M. Griffin, copy editor Tama Serfoss, Judy Gay Matthews for interior layout and design, and Debby Mattil and Barbara Ittner for their marketing expertise; Joan Garner for "The World of Ancient Beasts" map and other renderings; Professor Raymond P. Tripp, University of Denver, for his translations from the Old English of "The Old English Phoenix" and "Beowulf's Dragon Fight"; Beth Elder, Denver Public Library, for her reference leads into the vast area of children's literature; Kit Kederick, for sharing his knowledge of modern fantasy; Gary Reilly, for word processing assistance; Jim Nelson, for his natural history lore and proofing of the manuscript; and Esther Muzzillo, as always, for her classical sources and valuable suggestions throughout.

Acknowledgments

The author gratefully acknowledges permission to use the following copyrighted material, with special thanks to Edward Ormondroyd and Sheila G. Hancock.

"The Phoenix" from *The Metamorphoses* by Publius Ovidius Naso, translated by Horace Gregory. Translation © 1958 by The Viking Press, Inc., renewed 1986 by Patrick Bolton Gregory. Used with permission of Viking Penguin, a division of Penguin Books USA, Inc.

"The Phoenix of Arabia" and "The Wonder Beasts of Ethiopia" are reprinted by permission of the publishers and the Loeb Classical Library from Pliny the Elder, *Natural History*, Volume III, translated by H. Rackham. Cambridge, Mass.: Harvard University Press, 1983.

"The Old English Phoenix" was translated for this book by Raymond P. Tripp, Jr., © 1994 by the translator.

"Beowulf's Dragon Fight" from *Beowulf: An Edition and Literary Translation, In Progress*, edited and translated by Raymond P. Tripp, Jr., Denver, Colo.: The Society for New Language Study, 1990. Reprinted with minor editorial changes by permission of the translator.

"The Phoenix and the Falcon" is taken from *Russian Folk and Fairy Tales* by E. M. Almedingen. It was first published in the United States by G. P. Putnam's Sons, 1963. Copyright © 1957 by E. M. Almedingen. Reprinted by permission of the author through the author's agent, Sheil Land Associates.

"The Griffins of India" is reprinted by permission of the publishers and the Loeb Classical Library from Aelian's *On the Characteristics of Animals*, Volume I, translated by A. F. Scholfield. Cambridge, Mass.: Harvard University Press, 1971. Copyright © 1958 by the President and Fellows of Harvard College.

"The Griffon" from *Italian Fairy Tales*, retold by Peter Lum (Bettina Lum Crowe). London: Frederick Muller Ltd., 1963. First published in the United States by Follett Publishing Company, 1967. Copyright © 1963 by Peter Lum. And "Saijosen and the Phoenixes" from *Fabulous Beasts*, by Peter Lum. New York: Pantheon Books. Copyright © 1951 by Peter Lum. The editor and publisher, working through the author's agent, Curtis Brown, were unable to reach the author's estate for permission.

"David and the Phoenix" from *David and the Phoenix*, by Edward Ormondroyd. Chicago: Follett Publishing Company. Copyright © 1957 by Edward Ormondroyd. Reprinted by permission of the author.

"The Fair Maid and the Snow-White Unicorn" from *Folk Tales from Moor and Mountain* by Winifred Finlay. New York: Roy Publishers, Inc. Copyright © 1969 by Winifred Finlay. Reprinted by permission of the author's daughter, Sheila G. Hancock.

"Gift of the Unicorn" from *Tales the People Tell in China* by Robert Wyndham. New York: Julian Messner, a division of Simon & Schuster. Copyright © 1971 by Robert Wyndham. Reprinted by permission of Simon & Schuster.

"The Last Unicorns" by Edward D. Hoch from *100 Great Fantasy Short Short Stories*, edited by Isaac Asimov, Terry Carr, and Martin H. Greenberg. Garden City, N.Y.: Doubleday, 1984. Copyright © 1958 by Columbia Publications, Inc. Renewed by the author. Reprinted by permission of the author.

"A Dragon Hunt" is reprinted by permission of the publishers and the Loeb Classical Library from Philostratus, *The Life of Apollonius of Tyana*, translated by F. C. Conybeare. Cambridge, Mass.: Harvard University Press, 1960.

"Tale of the Computer That Fought a Dragon" from *The Cosmic Carnival of Stanislaw Lem: An Anthology of Entertaining Stories by the Modern Master of Science Fiction*, edited by Michael Kandel. New York: Continuum. Copyright © 1981 by the Continuum Publishing Corporation. Reprinted by permission of the publisher.

"The Griffin's Song" from *The Land of Forgotten Beasts* by Barbara Wersba. New York: Antheneum, 1964. Text copyright © 1964 by Barbara Wersba. Reprinted by permission of the author's agent, McIntosh & Otis.

The editor gratefully acknowledges Dover Publications, Inc., as the primary publishing source of the illustrations from heraldry and natural histories that appear in this book. Other illustrations come from Dover books and a variety of traditional sources. The Dover books used in this volume are: James Fairbairn's *Heraldic Crests* (1993), Arthur Charles Fox-Davies's *Heraldry* (1991), Konrad Gesner's *Curious Woodcuts of Fanciful and Real Beasts* (1971), Richard Huber's *Treasury of Fantastic and Mythological Creatures* (1981), and Henry Lewis Johnson's *Decorative Ornaments and Alphabets of the Renaissance* (1991).

Introduction

Sitting around the fire, we fell to talking about fantastic creatures. What strange beings the human imagination had concocted in past ages!

Satyajit Ray, *The Unicorn Expedition*

The glorious phoenix spreads its wings in a mural in the Phoenix, Arizona airport. The eagle-lion griffin stands majestically on business signs, belt buckles, and coats of arms. Pewter and glass unicorns prance in gift shop windows. Dragons roar in fantasy games. Images of ancient fantastic animals are all around us and in our imaginations.

To most of us, these four fabulous beasts and a host of their relatives are animals of fantasy, not of nature. Through most of history, though, it was a different story. From ancient times until only a few centuries ago, mixed and magical creatures were generally believed to share the sky, waters, and earth with actual animals. In a world filled with an astonishing variety of animal life, it wasn't easy to know which creatures were real and which ones were fabulous, mythical, or imaginary.

Ancient Monsters

Monsters may have first emerged from the fearful imagination of our most distant ancestors as these people witnessed the awesome power of nature. Larger than any beasts they had encountered, the wind moaned and the thunder roared. The eyes of lightning flashed. And the golden bird of the sun rose into the sky each day and nested each night.

Humans with the heads of jackals and hawks, winged bulls, and a host of other composite creatures took shape in the paintings and sculpture of the ancient Egyptians, Sumerians, Assyrians, and others.

The first generation of literary beasts was described in oral story and later appeared in written poetry. The bull-man Minotaur, snake-haired medusa, many-headed hydra, horse-man centaur, and the Chimera—with the head and body of a lion, a goat's head growing from its back, and a snake for a tail—were among the brood of monsters born of the classical imagination. Most of those grotesque creatures passed into the realm of myth during the development of early science in the ancient world.

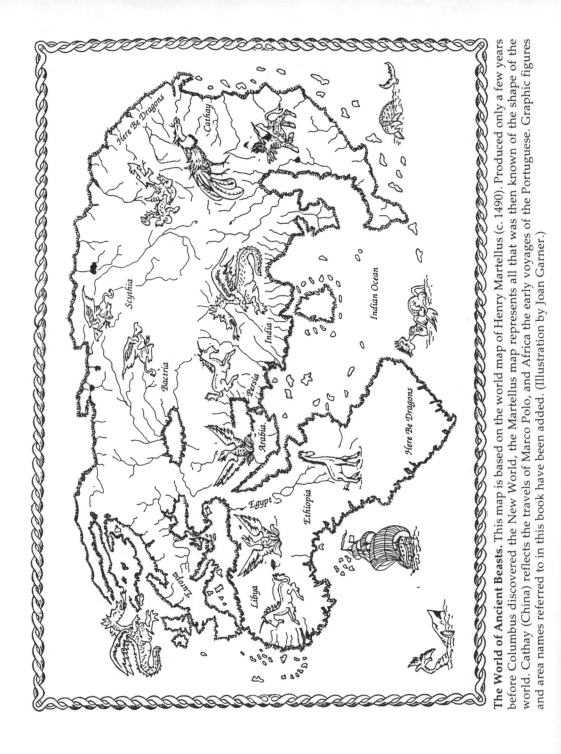

The World of Ancient Beasts. This map is based on the world map of Henry Martellus (c. 1490). Produced only a few years before Columbus discovered the New World, the Martellus map represents all that was then known of the shape of the world. Cathay (China) reflects the travels of Marco Polo, and Africa the early voyages of the Portuguese. Graphic figures and area names referred to in this book have been added. (Illustration by Joan Garner.)

Another set of beasts eventually took their place. The old monsters were only marvels, people thought, but the newer animals were different. Some people claimed to have seen these beasts with their own eyes; others simply accepted what they heard. And people heard about so many different kinds of animals they had never seen that anything seemed possible in the animal kingdom.

Early Travelers' Tales

Ancient travelers to Egypt, India, Ethiopia, Arabia, and Scythia returned to their own countries with tales of actual creatures so marvelous they seemed to come from dreams. Because no one back home had ever seen these animals, travelers compared the beasts to animals that were more familiar. Herodotus, the first major Western historian, described the Egyptian "river horse" as a four-legged animal as big as an ox, with cloven hoofs like an ox, the mane and tail of a horse, and voice like a horse's whinny. Another early writer, Ctesias, said the blood-red, man-eating manticore of India was as big as a lion, had a face, ears, and eyes like a man, had three rows of teeth, a long stinging tail like a scorpion, and a voice like a panpipe. One of the best-known mixed animals of ancient times was the camelopard. Some thought the spotted, long-necked creature was the offspring of a camel and a leopard. It was brown with white spots, had a neck like a horse, feet and legs like an ox, and a head like a camel.

Camelopards.

Today, we know the river horse as a hippopotamus and the camelopard as a giraffe. (The giraffe still carries the scientific name *Giraffa camelopardis*, and its starry counterpart is the Camelopardalis constellation.) The manticore was mostly imaginary, but was later identified with the Bengal tiger. No matter how common the animal is to the teller, the description of it will sound fantastic to the person who has never seen it.

And then there were the stories: An immortal bird that was continually reborn from its own ashes. A fierce, four-legged bird that guarded gold and jewels in its mountain nest. A beast as big as a horse with a single magical horn that could cure sickness. And great serpents that would shake the earth and fly over the sea, seeking ships to destroy. Other stories told of the rooster with a serpent's tail and a crown on its head with a look that would turn other living things to stone. Birds so gigantic that their wings blotted out the sun. And sea monsters so large that mariners landed on them, thinking they were islands.

Manticore.

Herodotus, Ctesias, Pliny, Aelian, and other early writers of history, geography, and science told stories of these animals in their books. Not all the writers thought the stories were true, but they told them anyway because they were good stories. Their accounts, in turn, were repeated by other writers down the centuries.

A monstrous whale.

Bestiaries

Christianity accepted many of the wonder beasts. The phoenix, griffin, unicorn, dragon, and others all appear in different translations of the Bible. They are also common in Christian art, in cathedral sculpture, and illuminated manuscripts.

The wonder beasts are mixed in with common creatures in the bestiaries of the medieval writers, books derived from what was called the *Physiologus* ("the book of nature" or "the naturalist"). Popular for centuries and translated into many languages from Icelandic to Arabic, bestiaries used stories about animals to teach moral and religious lessons. The ant and the bee were industrious, the crocodile and the fox devious, and the hedgehog prudent. The whale who dragged sailors to their doom was evil, and the unicorn and phoenix represented goodness and rebirth. Whether any particular animal was real was not as important as the vice or virtue it illustrated. The ancient wonder beasts also appeared in medieval encyclopedias.

Heraldry

While some scholars doubted the existence of one or more of the wonder beasts, the creatures thrived in medieval heraldry and are prominent in coats of arms to this day.

In the Middle Ages, heraldry developed into the systematic use of symbols to represent individuals and families as crests, on shields, and on the banners of knights. Animals in heraldry were often pictured like travelers' hybrid descriptions of old. Horses sprouted wings like mythical Pegasus, and along with lions and other animals they grew fish tails. (It was commonly believed that land animals had their counterparts in the sea—such as the sea horse, or hippocampus, the lion of the sea, and sea dog.) In heraldry, beasts signified qualities of nobility, courage, and strength, and were identified with the most highly respected people and institutions on earth.

Heraldic hippocampus.

The fabulous animal most often portrayed on coats of arms was the griffin. The griffin, the unicorn, and the dragon are still among the most common figures in heraldry.

Lion of the Sea.

Later Travelers' Tales

Meanwhile, travelers from the Western world were venturing beyond what they knew to lands as strange as fantasy. Early maps depicted many creatures that were strange to those who were familiar mostly with farm and domestic animals. Some of the beasts on maps had long noses, others long necks, some had humps on their backs. And often among the elephants, giraffes, and camels were four-legged creatures with wings, giant snakes with legs, and monsters rising from the seas, ready to swallow ships that ventured far from shore.

During the Crusades of the twelfth century, copies and translations of a letter from a distant priest-king appeared across Europe. The writer, whoever he was, fictitiously called himself Prester John, Emperor of India. Giants, pygmies, one-eyed people, black and green unicorns, brightly colored bears and lions, griffins, a dragon, and the one and only phoenix lived in his land of marvels. The kingdom of Prester John is depicted on many early maps.

Prester John's fabled empire became so famous that Europeans traveling to far parts of the world commonly looked for his realm. About the same time that the Letter of Prester John was originally circulated, a real traveler, Rabbi Benjamin of Tudela, described the people of Prester John as being noseless people who lived in the wilderness. In his famous book of travels, Marco Polo, too, refers to Prester John, telling the story of how the legendary emperor was killed in a battle with Genghis Khan. Much of the letter shows up again in the renowned *Travels* of Sir John Mandeville. Like the writer of the Prester John letter, Mandeville probably did most of his traveling in his own library, collecting material from the ancient writers as well as stories from his own time. The books of both Marco Polo and Sir John Mandeville were used in mapping distant lands, and Christopher Columbus carried a copy of Mandeville's book along with him on his voyage to the New World.

Many sailors reported seeing mermaids frolicking in the sea, and adventurers wrote of either seeing or hearing about animals we now regard as fantastic. Rabbi Benjamin of Tudela wrote of sailors in the Far East who tricked griffins to save themselves from sinking ships. The Moroccan Ibn Battuta encountered what native sailors believed to be the gigantic rukh (roc), and Lewis Vartoman described unicorns in the temple of Mecca and in the city of Zeila. Marco Polo, though, pointed out that tropical unicorns (rhinoceroses) were not the graceful, mysterious animals that Europeans imagined them to be and that the "gryphon birds" of Madagascar were not the fabled eagle-lion beasts that guard gold in remote mountains.

The Scholars

While European explorers were sailing around the globe discovering new lands, peoples, and animals, astronomers explored the heavens through telescopes, and scholars rediscovered books of the past. The printing press and translations of works from Greek and Latin made books accessible to more people.

Dürer's rhinoceros.

Many Renaissance scholars who wrote about animals simply repeated the lore of the ancient writers such as Herodotus and Pliny. Some compiled voluminous works of natural history, gathering everything known about the animals of the world. Those early printed books, such as Konrad Gesner's *History of Animals* (1552), were heavily illustrated. Many of the pictures, including several in this book, are still well-known. Among those illustrations are Albrecht Dürer's armored rhinoceros, the unicorn, the dragon, and sea monsters from Olaus Magnus's book on fish of the northern seas.

Edward Topsell translated Gesner's work into English in his *Historie of Foure-Footed Beasts* (1658; 1962), in which he added much material of his own. His book includes a long chapter defending the reality of the unicorn, and he presents the manticore, the dragon, and many other animals from fable and legend as real creatures. Printed in the century that saw the rise of modern science, Topsell's book was one of the last to include wondrous beasts among the world's animals.

The fortunes of wonder beasts changed drastically in the seventeenth century. For thousands of years, they had generally been accepted because the great writers of the past had included them in their books. A new scientific spirit in the 1600s, though, encouraged scholars to question ancient authority. The ideas of Pliny and others could now be attacked, and with them the animals they wrote about.

Sir Thomas Browne's *Vulgar Errors* (1646) represented a turning point in the history of the wonder animals. True to the spirit of its time, the book attacked many traditional truths. Among those were beliefs in the griffin, the phoenix, the two-headed amphisbaena, the magic of unicorn horn, and the story of a basilisk egg being laid by a rooster and hatched by a toad. Alexander Ross, a once well-known writer and schoolmaster, championed tradition and the ancient writers, but his views could not stand up against the New Science. By the end of the seventeenth century, fabulous creatures were finally separated from the other animals and scorned as fantastic figments of the imagination.

Except for their being a part of heraldry, the wonder beasts of the West seemed all but forgotten for 200 years.

Return of the Wonder Beasts

In Asia and other parts of the world, though, the major wonder beasts and their relatives lived on. Since ancient times, the phoenix, unicorn, and dragon—along with the tortoise—have been among the four celestial animals of China, and in one country after another, imaginary animals were alive and well in art, folktales, and fairy tales.

Western artists and philosophers of the early 1800s, revolting against the Age of Reason, glorified the imagination where wonder beasts had lived all along. The English poet William Wordsworth declared that the material world of the Industrial Revolution was "too much with us." He longed to be "A Pagan in a creed outworn/Have glimpses that would make me less forlorn/Have sight of Proteus rising from the sea/Or hear old Triton blow his wreathed horn."

New interest in mythology, legend, and folktale unearthed stories forgotten or ignored, and imaginary creatures reappeared as characters in children's literature and fantasy. Also, paleontologists unearthed bones of prehistoric creatures, leading some to believe that dragons and unicorns might have lived during the dawn of life on the planet.

One who thought so was Charles Gould, geologist and member of the Royal Society of Tasmania. His 1886 book, *Mythical Monsters*, must have given hope to those who fervently wished that wonder beasts were real. Gould believed that the unicorn and other fantastic animals perished in the great Flood. He proposed that

> many of the so-called mythical animals, which throughout long ages and in all nations have been the fertile subjects of fiction and fable, come legitimately within the scope of plain matter-of-fact Natural History, and that they may be considered, not as the outcome of exuberant fancy, but as creatures which really once existed, and of which, unfortunately, only imperfect and inaccurate descriptions have filtered down to us, probably very much refracted, through the mists of time.

There were frequent reports of unicorns seen in central Africa. Many ships' captains claimed they saw sea serpents, and later, in the 1920s, expeditions were formed in Southeast Asia to find the terrible dragons of Komodo.

The bones of primordial creatures turned out to be those of dinosaurs and mammoths no less awesome than animals of the imagination. The single horns of the unicorns of Africa might well have been created artificially. Sea serpents were generally explained as mistaken observation, and the Komodo dragons were large lizards.

Today, we are still fascinated by tales of Bigfoot (or Sasquatch) in the forests of the northwest United States; an Abominable Snowman (or Yeti) up in the snowy Himalayas; and a sea monster in the depths of Scotland's Loch Ness. Many people say they have actually seen those creatures, and evidence of various kinds—from casts of footprints to photographs—has been presented to prove that the beasts are real.

The 1994 revelation that the famous 1934 photograph of the Loch Ness monster, Nessie, was a fake is only the latest fabulous-beast hoax to be exposed. There have been many such hoaxes through the ages. Unicorn horns displayed in cathedrals and museums were usually tusks of the narwhal, sometimes called "the unicorn of the sea." Griffin claws were ibex horns set in gold or silver. Monstrous Jenny Hanivers were dried ray fish twisted into grotesque shapes. The birds of paradise that Europeans took back with them from Indonesia were fabled to live in air because the prepared specimens were legless. In our time, an entertaining television documentary showed a man making Bigfoot tracks in the snow with snowshoe-like feet. Even joke Montana jackalopes (jackrabbits with antelope horns attached) have been known to confound overseas customs officers.

Hoaxes, though, are only one explanation for the sources of imaginary animals. Since the late 1800s, scholars have offered several others. Wonder beasts, we now think, were born from travelers' exotic tales and illustrations of animals, from inaccurate observation, from ancient bones, from fears of the unknown, and from the imagination's sheer delight in creating new beasts.

The Renaissance artist Albrecht Dürer said that if an artist wants "to create the stuff that dreams are made of, let him freely mix all sorts of creatures." The desire—maybe need—to combine the powers of different animals into a new creature is as old as humankind and as recent as the latest fantasy movie filled with strange animal forms. Whatever it was that made people interested in imaginary animals through the ages is still part of us today.

Among the host of fabulous animals in art and story, the phoenix, griffin, unicorn, and dragon enjoy an honored place. All four have been identified with constellations, and all except the griffin are among the celestial animals of China. This collection of tales and lore follows them from ancient histories right up to children's literature and modern fantasy. These wonder beasts and their relatives take us around the world and through time.

The Phoenix

The Phoenix

he fabled phoenix is a crimson, gold, and purple bird with sweeping tail and jeweled eyes. It lives in a distant garden of flowers and crystal springs. When its wings become heavy with age, the bird builds a nest of spices, herbs, and resin in the top of a date palm. The heat of the sun ignites the twigs, and the phoenix stands in the flames with outspread wings. The bird burns to ashes. In cool starlight, a young phoenix forms in the remains of its parent. The reborn bird rises with the rising sun and spreads its bright new wings to greet the day. It flies high with youthful strength, followed by all the birds of the air. Its own parent and its own child, the only one of its kind in the world, the aged phoenix dies and is reborn over and over again, through all eternity.

This version of the story is the most common in our time. The Western phoenix lives and dies in many ways in different versions, and its life cycle varies from story to story, from 100 years to thousands. The bird's legendary counterparts in China and Japan never die at all, but live in the Land of the Immortals.

From its ancient beginnings, though, the phoenix has always been likened to the sun. The shining bird of fable forever renews itself like the sun, dying fiery red at the end of the day and rising golden the next morning. Greatest of mythical birds, the phoenix is the triumphant symbol of rebirth and renewal of the human spirit.

The Phoenix from the Past

The mysterious beginnings of the phoenix (also fenix or phenix) can be seen in its very name, a Greek word that also means "purple-red," "crimson," "date," "date palm," and "Phoenicia." The date palm continually renews itself, and Phoenicia is "the red land." Together, the several words suggest that the bird is associated with red and purple and comes from the East, land of the sunrise. Traditionally, the phoenix has been sacred to the sun.

Phoenix was the name Greek writers gave the Egyptian *bennu*, a symbol of the gods Ra and Osiris and a hieroglyph representing the sun. The *bennu* introduces itself in the Egyptian *Book of the Dead*: "I am bennu, that which is in Heliopolis. I am the keeper of the book of that which is, and of that which shall be." This stork or heron figure would not seem to be the eagle-like bird the Greek historian Herodotus saw in Egyptian paintings, but he did report that it was worshipped in Heliopolis, "the City of the Sun."

Versions of the Story

A *bennu* bird.

Like the mythical bird itself, the phoenix appears and reappears in books down the centuries. Typical of stories that grow over time, details of the death and rebirth of the phoenix change from one account to another. Herodotus reported only that the reborn phoenix bears the dead parent to the Temple of the Sun in a ball of myrrh. The Roman poet Ovid wrote that the new bird rises from the breast of the old in a nest of spices built in the highest branches of a palm tree, and that the young bird carries nest and all to the Temple of the Sun. As Pliny recorded, a maggot is born from the bones of the older bird and grows into the younger phoenix. The Roman historian Tacitus said that the dying bird builds a nest and "infuses into it a germ of life."

As the phoenix fable changes over time, fire eventually becomes a part of the tale. In a fourth-century Latin poem by Lactantius, the older phoenix bursts into flame from the heat of its glowing body and the sun and burns to ashes in its nest of spices. Several centuries later, in the mythical kingdom of Prester John, the phoenix catches fire because it flies too close to the sun. In other versions, the nest of aromatic spices bursts into flame from the sun's heat or from the fanning of the bird's wings.

The life span of the phoenix, too, changes from one version to another, even though the most common number is 500 years. The Greek writer Aelian lightheartedly said the phoenix did not have to count on its fingers to know when it was time to be reborn, because it was so close to nature that it just knew. The 540 years Pliny cites is the period of the Great Year, the time it takes for stars and planets to revolve through an entire cycle. The belief was that because human life was so affected by the position of the planets, history repeats itself through each cycle of the Great Year, just as the phoenix does. The life cycle of the phoenix in other versions of the story varies from 100 years to 12,954 years.

A Roman Story

The gluttonous Roman Emperor Heliogabalus, who named himself after a sun god, liked exotic meals. He ordered his cooks to mix gold and gems in his food, and he savored the brains and tongues of birds. Thinking he could become immortal by feasting on the one and only phoenix, Heliogabalus sent his men to the ends of the world to find the rare bird. One envoy returned from the Far East with a brilliantly colored creature with long, sweeping tail feathers. Shortly after devouring the delicacy, the Emperor was murdered, leading many to suggest that what he ate was a bird of paradise, but obviously not the immortal phoenix.

The Phoenix of the Middle Ages

Like many of the other wonder beasts, the phoenix entered a new stage of its history in the Middle Ages. The phoenix is referred to in some translations of the Bible, as when Job says, "In my nest I shall die and like the phoenix extend my days." Church fathers regarded the death and rebirth of the phoenix as an allegory of Christ's Resurrection, and the bird is commonly treated in the bestiaries as a symbol of Christ. The Old English poem, "The Phoenix," based on the Roman poem by Lactantius is a colorful retelling of the story with Christian overtones.

Bestiary phoenix. (Illustration by Joan Garner.)

The Phoenix in Heraldry

Heraldic phoenix.

The image of the phoenix in heraldry is one of the reasons we think of the bird having outspread wings, seeming to rise from a nest of fire. The heraldic bird that represents the phoenix is the eagle, which reminds us that Herodotus said the phoenix he saw in Egyptian paintings resembled an eagle in shape and size. A phoenix in flames—with the motto, "Her death itself will make her live"—was used as a symbol for the warrior maiden Joan of Arc, who was burned at the stake for heresy and became a martyr. Also, Queen Elizabeth I of England, who had been imprisoned in the Tower of London before becoming queen, used the phoenix as her heraldic emblem.

Discounted by Scholars

In his book, *Vulgar Errors* (1646), Sir Thomas Browne declared there were so many versions of the phoenix story, so many different numbers for its life span, and so many different details of its death and rebirth, that no one could believe any of them. Besides, science had proven that no bird could be immortal. Alexander Ross, called the "Champion of the Ancients," defended the phoenix against Browne's attack, but to no avail. A few years later, a German scholar, George Caspard Kirchmayer, wrote:

> This creature is quite a myth, and has never been seen except in pictures (I used the words of Herodotus). No man has ever seen it in true reality. Except a " 'tis said," " 'tis reported," " 'tis a tale," or "so they say," no one can bring forward a clear statement in regard to the matter. I regard as impossible, absurd, and openly ridiculous whatever, except in the way of a fiction, has been told of this creature. Such a belief as that in the phoenix is a slander against Holy Writ, nature, and sound reason.

Faced with such a hostile world, the Western phoenix withdrew to the land of fable.

Heraldic phoenix.

The Sacred Phoenix of Egypt

Herodotus

The Greek traveler and historian Herodotus [Heh-ROD-uh-tus], circa 484-425 B.C., is known as the "Father of History." Much of his History *is derived from what he saw and heard during his many years of travel around the ancient world. He heard the phoenix story in Egypt. It is the first major account we have of the magical bird.*

hey have also another sacred bird called the phoenix, which I myself have never seen, except in pictures. Indeed it is a great rarity, even in Egypt, only coming there—according to the accounts of the people of Heliopolis—once in five hundred years, when the old phoenix dies. Its size and appearance, if it is like the pictures, are as follows:— The plumage is partly red, partly golden, while the general make and size are almost exactly that of the eagle. They tell a story of what this bird does, which does not seem to me to be credible; that he comes all the way from Arabia, and brings the parent bird, all plastered over with myrrh, to the temple of the Sun, and there buries the body. In order to bring him, they say, he first forms a ball of myrrh as big as he finds that he can carry; then he hollows out the ball, and puts his parent inside, after which he covers over the opening with fresh myrrh, and the ball is then of exactly the same weight as at first; so he brings it to Egypt, plastered over as I have said, and deposits it in the temple of the Sun. Such is the story they tell of the doings of this bird.

From *The History of Herodotus*, translated by George Rawlinson. New York: D. Appleton, 1859.

The Phoenix

The Phoenix

Ovid

Hundreds of years after Herodotus recounted the death and rebirth of the phoenix, the Roman poet Ovid [AH-vid], 43 B.C.-A.D. 18, included a variation of the story in his Metamorphoses, *a collection of classical myths about the changing forms of gods, goddesses, humans, and animals. This tale is told by "the Philosopher."*

othing retains the shape of what it was,
And Nature, always making old things new,
Proves nothing dies within the universe,
But takes another being in new forms.
What is called birth is change from what we were,
And death the shape of being left behind.
Though all things melt or grow from here to there,
Yet the same balance of the world remains.

* * *

"How many creatures walking on this earth
Have their first being in another form?
Yet one exists that is itself forever,
Reborn in ageless likeness through the years.
It is that bird Assyrians call the Phoenix,
Nor does he eat the common seeds and grasses,
But drinks the juice of rare, sweet-burning herbs.
When he has done five hundred years of living
He winds his nest high up a swaying palm—
And delicate dainty claws prepare his bed
Of bark and spices, myrrh and cinnamon—
And dies while incense lifts his soul away.

Then from his breast—or so the legend runs—
A little Phoenix rises over him,
To live, they say, the next five hundred years.
When he is old enough in hardihood,
He lifts his crib (which is his father's tomb)
Midair above the tall palm wavering there
And journeys toward the city of the Sun,
Where in Sun's temple shines the Phoenix' nest."

From *The Metamorphoses* by Ovid. Translated by Horace Gregory. New York: Viking Press, pp. 421, 425-26. Copyright © 1958 by The Viking Press, renewed 1986 by Patrick Bolton Gregory.

The Phoenix of Arabia

Pliny the Elder

The Natural History of Pliny the Elder [PLIH-nee], A.D. 23-79, is a treasure house of wonder beast lore. Pliny's account of the phoenix's birth and reported appearance in Egypt is one of the best-known versions of the tale. In classical times, "Ethiopia" was the generic name for the area south of Egypt; "Indies" was the name for India and Asia. "A.U.C." is the abbreviation of a Latin phrase meaning "from the founding of the city." Pliny died in the eruption of Mount Vesuvius when he went to investigate the phenomenon and to rescue friends.

hey say that Ethiopia and the Indies possess birds extremely variegated in colour and indescribable, and that Arabia has one that is famous before all others (though perhaps it is fabulous), the phoenix, the only one in the whole world and hardly ever seen. The story is that it is as large as an eagle, and has a gleam of gold round its neck and all the rest of it is purple, but the tail blue picked out with rose-coloured feathers and the throat picked out with tufts, and a feathered crest adorning its head. The first and the most detailed Roman account of it was given by Manilius, the eminent senator famed for his extreme and varied learning acquired without a teacher: he stated that nobody has ever existed that has seen one feeding, that in Arabia it is sacred to the Sun-god, that it lives 540 years, that when it is growing old it constructs a nest with sprigs of wild cinnamon and frankincense, fills it with scents and lies on it till it dies; that subsequently from its bones and marrow is born first a sort of maggot, and this grows into a chicken, and that this begins by paying due funeral rites to the former bird and carrying the whole nest down to the City of the Sun near Panchaia and depositing it upon an altar there. Manilius also states that the period of the Great Year coincides with the life of this bird, and that the same indications of the seasons and stars return again, and that this begins about noon on the day on which the sun enters the sign of the Ram, and that the year of this period had been 215, as reported by him, in the consulship of Publius Licinius and Gnaeus Cornelius. Cornelius Valerianus reports that a phoenix flew down into Egypt in the consulship of Quintus Plautius and Sextus Papinius; it was even brought to Rome in the Censorship of the Emperor Claudius, A.U.C. 800 and displayed in the Comitium, a fact attested by the Records, although nobody would doubt that this phoenix was a fabrication.

From *Natural History*, Volume III, by Pliny the Elder. Translated by H. Rackham, Cambridge, Mass.: Harvard University Press, 1983, pp. 293, 295.

The Phoenix Appears in Egypt

Tacitus

In his Annals, *a history of Rome, Tacitus [TA-cih-tus], circa A.D. 55-120, tells of another report of the phoenix being seen in Egypt. That recorded appearance of the sacred bird was in the period A.D. 32-37, during the reign of the emperor Tiberius. Tacitus was the first writer to mention the birds that accompany the phoenix in its flight.*

uring the consulship of Paulus Fabius and Lucius Vitellius, the bird called the phoenix, after a long succession of ages, appeared in Egypt and furnished the most learned men of that country and of Greece with abundant matter for the discussion of the marvelous phenomenon. It is my wish to make known all on which they agree with several things, questionable enough indeed, but not too absurd to be noticed.

That it is a creature sacred to the sun, differing from all other birds in its beak and in the tints of its plumage, is held unanimously by those who have described its nature. As to the number of years it lives, there are various accounts. The general tradition says five hundred years. Some maintain that it is seen at intervals of fourteen hundred and sixty-one years, and that the former birds flew into the city called Heliopolis successively in the reigns of Sesostris, Amasis, and Ptolemy, the third king of the Macedonian dynasty, with a multitude of companion birds marveling at the novelty of the appearance. But all antiquity is of course obscure. From Ptolemy to Tiberius was a period of less than five hundred years. Consequently some have supposed that this was a spurious phoenix, not from the regions of Arabia, and with none of the instincts which ancient tradition has attributed to the bird. For when the number of years is completed and death is near, the phoenix, it is said, builds a nest in the land of its birth and infuses into it a germ of life from which an offspring arises, whose first care, when fledged, is to bury its father. This is not rashly done, but taking up a load of myrrh and having tried its strength by a long flight, as soon as it is equal to the burden and to the journey, it carries its father's body, bears it to the Altar of the Sun, and leaves it to the flames. All this is full of doubt and legendary exaggeration. Still, there is no question that the bird is occasionally seen in Egypt.

From *The Annals of Tacitus*, translated by Alfred John Church and William Jackson Brodribb. London: Macmillan, 1877.

The Old English Phoenix

Old English Poem

This lush medieval retelling of the phoenix fable comes from the tenth-century Exeter Book. *These excerpts from "The Phoenix" were translated for* Wonder Beasts *by Raymond P. Tripp, Jr.*

hen the wind drops, and weather is fair,
When the bright holy gem of heaven shines
In a clear sky, the restless waters
Stand still, and every storm is put
To sleep from the sky, and from the south
The warm sun makes sweet light for men,
Then in the branches the Phoenix begins
To make his nest. Great need he has
To see if he can turn old age quickly
Through the fire of knowledge back into life
And be young again. Then from far and near
He collects and carries the sweetest
Of delightful herbs and forest blossoms

To his dwelling, each noble fragrance
Of the spicy herbs which the World-King,
The Father of everything upon earth, has made
So they contain every kind of essence,
Sweet under the sky. He himself carries
These bright treasures into his tree.
There this wild bird builds his house,
Bright and delightful, and there lodges
In its upper room and in that leafy shade
Surrounds his body and feathers
On every side with holy fragrances
And the noblest blossoms of earth.
And eager there he sits. When the sun,
The gem of the summer sky, the hottest,
Pierces the shadows and, tracing its course,
Lights up the world, then his house
Grows hot in the heat of the bright sky,
Herbs grow warm, his pleasant house begins
To emit sweet odors, then both bird and nest
Burst into flames in the embrace of fire.
The pyre is lit. Flame rolls over
His house of flesh, and fiercely clinging
Yellow fire feeds on the burning Phoenix,
Old with many years. The fire devours
His mortal body—life is on a journey
From that fated breast. The funeral flames
Set flesh and bone on fire, but after a while
A new life comes back into him again.
After his ashes cool, he once more begins
After the fury of flame to come together,
Clinging to a shape. Then clean is
The brightest of nests, consumed by the fire
The brave bird's hall. His body cools,
His bone-house crumbles, and burning subsides.
Then out of the pyre looking like an apple,
Something in the ashes is once more seen,
A thing growing into a worm, wondrously fair,
As from an egg it were freshly hatched,
Shiny wet from its shell. Then in the shade
He grows, at first, like an eagle's chick,
A handsome young bird; then further yet

His beauty swells, taking the joyous shape
Of a mature eagle, and after that at last,
Dressed in feathers as he was before,
He blossoms into brightness.

* * *

His brave front is a marvel of color,
Variously shaded about the breast.
The back of his head is green,
Handsomely varied and blended with purple.
His tail as well is brilliantly parted,
Dark and shiny, scarlet, bright with spots,
All artfully spaced. His feathers are
White toward the back, and his neck green
Down low and up high, and his bill sparkles
Like glass or gems, while his jaws glisten
Inside and out. The look of his eyes is
Fierce and of a stony hue, honed like
Some polished gem set in a golden cup
And worked by a clever jeweler's craft.
Around his neck is, like a ring of sun,
A flashing circle fashioned of feathers.
A wonder is his body below, so fair,
Sheer, and shining. A feathered crest
Joins artful patterns all along his back.
His legs are armed with golden plates,
His feet are tawny bronze. This bird shines
In every way unique, most like a peacock,
Endowed with happy features, as books say.
He is never slow, sluggish, nor hesitating,
Never heavy plodding, like other birds,
When they feather slowly through the air.
But he is quick, swift, and very light,
Bright, beautiful, and marked by wonder.

The Old English Phoenix, edited and translated by Raymond P. Tripp, Jr. Denver, Colo.: The Society for New Language Study, 1994. Copyright © 1994 by Raymond P. Tripp, Jr.

The Phoenix Around the World

The phoenix appears in many variations in stories around the world. Also, besides its Asian counterparts, there are several distant cousins of the bird, related by common characteristics.

The Feng Huang

With the dragon, the unicorn, and the tortoise, the phoenix (Feng Huang) is one of the four celestial animals of China. Each one governs one of the quadrants of the heavens. The phoenix, associated with the sun, presides over the southern quadrant. It is regarded as the emperor of the 360 classes of birds.

The Feng Huang, or Chinese phoenix. (From *Mythical Monsters* by Charles Gould.)

The Feng Huang nests in the wu t'ung (dryandra) tree far away in the K'unlun Mountains and appears to mankind only in times of peace. At other times, one can play a stringed instrument under a wu t'ung tree in hopes that the Feng Huang will appear and add its song to the music.

Like the Western phoenix, the Feng Huang is immortal, and all the birds of the earth follow its flight in homage. Unlike its Western counterpart, the Feng Huang is regarded as two birds, the male (Feng) and the female (Huang), who neither die nor are reborn but live eternally in the Land of the Immortals. Together, they represent eternal love.

The long tail of the Feng Huang is as bright as fire, and its plumage is symbolic of various virtues, a blend of red (uprightness), azure (humanity), yellow (virtue), white (honesty), and black (sincerity). Some say the Feng Huang resembles the Argus pheasant and the peacock. Others say it is a hybrid of other animals, including the swan, the unicorn, the dragon, and the tortoise. The bird's song is said to be the source of the Chinese musical scale.

Born of the sun, the Feng Huang was sacred to the royal family, and its figure was embroidered on the robes of the empresses of China. Its first appearance was first recorded around 2600 B.C. during the reign of Hung Ti, and the bird was later reported seen during the reigns of several other ancient emperors.

The Ho-ho

The phoenix of Japan is the Ho-ho (Ho-o), which only rarely leaves its heavenly home and descends to earth as a sign of peace and love.

The Cinnamon Bird

This Arabian bird, also known as the Cinomolgus, is similar to the Western phoenix in that it builds its nest from spices. It figures in a story that explains the origin of cinnamon, an exotic spice once as valuable as gold. Herodotus said no one knows what country these large birds bring the spice from, but that they use mud to attach their nests made from cinnamon sticks to cliff faces. To get the cinnamon, people cut up the carcasses of their beasts of burden and place the meat at the base of the cliffs where the cinnamon birds live. The birds carry the meat to their nests, but the food is so heavy that the nests fall to the ground. The people then collect the cinnamon and sell it to merchants from other countries.

The Ilerion

While only one phoenix lives at a time, there are two Ilerion (Allerion, Ylerion) in the world at a time. Prester John wrote in his famous letter that after the male and female Ilerion live sixty years, they build a nest. The female lays two eggs and sits on them for forty days. When the young are born, the parent birds—accompanied by all the birds of the land—fly to the sea, where the Ilerion drown themselves. The other birds return to the nest and feed the young Ilerion until they are old enough to nurture themselves.

Salamandra

The ancient Arabs believed the fire-resistant material asbestos was the plumage of a phoenix-like bird they called Salamandra. Prester John said in his letter that asbestos was a cloth spun from the silkworm-like covering of the salamander, a lizard that according to fable lived in fire.

The Bird of Paradise

Also known as Manucodiata, "Bird of the Gods," this bird is often compared to the phoenix because of its brilliant plumage and its long, resplendent tail feathers. It is said to be born in paradise, like the Chinese Feng Huang and the Japanese Ho-ho. Footless, it spends its life in air, drinking the dew of heaven, until it dies and drops to earth.

The Greek philosopher Aristotle said there could be no birds without feet, but the Malaysian bird of paradise is scientifically named *Paradisea apoda* (without feet). Europeans who sailed to the Orient returned with the brightly colored but seemingly legless birds, which natives had skinned and stuck onto sticks.

The Firebird

A magical bird of Russian folklore, this crested creature with jeweled eyes and shining feathers steals golden apples from the royal garden. The Tsar offered his kingdom to whichever of his three sons was able to bring the bird to him. Only the youngest, Ivan, did not fall asleep while guarding the tree of golden apples and managed to pluck a feather from the bird's tail. After pursuing the bird through many adventures, Ivan returned home, inherited the kingdom, and married a beautiful royal maiden.

There are many variations of this tale, sometimes called "The Firebird," sometimes "Prince Ivan and the Gray Wolf." Music lovers are familiar with this fiery bird through Stravinsky's ballet, *The Firebird*.

The Phoenixes Are Flying

Chinese Ode

In China, the appearance of a pair of phoenixes has traditionally been regarded as a sign of good government and prosperity in the land. The Chinese philosopher Confucius (c. 551-478 B.C.), who died about the time Herodotus was born, expressed how discouraged he was with his own times when he wrote that the phoenix did not appear. In these verses from an ode from the ancient Shih King [Shih Ching], *the poet praises his ruler by implying that times are so good that the phoenixes are ready to descend to earth.*

he male and female phoenix fly about,
Their wings rustling,
When they settle in their proper resting-place.
Many are your admirable officers, O king,
Ready to be employed by you,
Loving you, the Son of Heaven.

The male and female phoenix fly about,
Their wings rustling,
As they soar up to heaven.
Many are your admirable officers, O king,
Waiting for your commands,
And loving the multitudes of the people.

The male and female phoenix give out their notes,
On that lofty ridge.
The dryandras grow,
On those eastern slopes.
They grow luxuriantly;
And harmoniously the notes resound.

Adapted from *The Sacred Books of China*, translated by James Legge. Oxford: Clarendon Press, 1879, p. 406.

Saijosen and the Phoenixes

Japanese Fairy Tale

Like the Chinese Feng Huang, the Japanese Ho-Ho only rarely descends to earth from its heavenly home. Both were figures embroidered on the robes of empresses. In this tale retold by Peter Lum (Bettina Lum Crowe) in her classic book, Fabulous Beasts, *phoenixes appear to a Japanese maiden.*

t is told how long ago a young girl named Saijosen one day busied herself with her embroidery. Her skill at this work was great, and she was renowned for the figures of men and gods and beasts that she wove into tapestry so cleverly that they seemed to have been living creatures caught in the silk. As she sat there on this particular day, she suddenly became aware of an elderly man standing beside her. When she looked up he spoke no word of greeting but pointed to a space in the embroidery.

"Work for me there the shape of two phoenixes," he said, and she was so surprised that she immediately began the design as he told her.

This strange visitor stood waiting and watching while she worked, which was almost the whole day. No sooner were the two birds complete in all their sunset coloring than their wings trembled and they lifted themselves from the cloth. Then the old man mounted on the back of one phoenix, motioning Saijosen to do the same, and the two soared away to the land of the immortals, never to be seen again.

The Phoenix and the Falcon

Russian Fairy Tale

This story from E. M. Almedingen's Russian Folk and Fairy Tales *combines the magic of fairy tales with traditional lore of the fabulous bird.*

any, many years ago in a big town there lived a widowed merchant who had an only daughter, and he cherished her as though she were the apple of his eye.

Once, about to go to a fair in a distant town, he asked her, "Well, Child, and what would you like for a present from the fair this time? Shall I bring you a dress of crimson silk or a pair of yellow shoes or a string of corals?"

To his surprise, she did not answer all at once but began folding a towel she had been hemming.

"What?" the merchant said in surprise. "Are you tired of finery, then? Don't you want me to bring you anything at all?"

The young girl shook her head.

"Indeed I do, but there was a dream I dreamt a few nights ago—"

He stared at her.

"What's a dream got to do with it?" he asked her.

"Father, it was a most important dream."

"Well, then, tell me all about it. Were you dreaming about a pearl necklace? I might be able to afford it. You know," he added warmly, "there is nothing I would refuse you."

"I wish I could tell you all about it," said the girl, "but when I woke up I had forgotten it all except the end. Please, Father, could you bring me a feather of Phoenix the Great Bird?"

"Phoenix the Great Bird? Why, Child, what a thing to ask for! I don't think I've ever heard about such a bird. Is it some kind of a falcon?"

"I don't know," said the girl sadly. "Indeed, Father, I know no more than you do, but it is so important that I should be given one such feather."

"I'll try," the merchant told her, "but I wish you knew why such a thing should be important."

Off he went, and reached the great city where the annual fair was held. His own business finished, the merchant began looking for a feather of Phoenix the Great Bird. He first went into the street where canaries, parrots and paradise birds were sold in magnificent gilt and jeweled cages. But not a man there could tell him anything about Phoenix the Great Bird. Someone advised the merchant to try the alley where falcons might be bought.

"Such a bird may indeed belong to their species. It may well be some foreign falcon or other."

So the merchant spent a whole morning among the sellers of falcons, and at last he came into a small dim shop where a very old man, on hearing his request, shook his head.

"Indeed, Phoenix the Great Bird is not a falcon."

"But does such a bird exist at all?" asked the bewildered merchant. "I have not met a single man who had ever heard of it."

"Exist at all?" The old man smiled. "My dear sir, it is a king of birds. Why, it is above any eagle in dignity and beauty."

The merchant looked even more bewildered.

"And why should it be so?" he wanted to know.

"Because an eagle is hatched and fledged. It lives its appointed span and it dies. A phoenix leaps into the fire, is burned to ashes, and then rises again more beautiful than before. But you will never find any such bird on sale anywhere. Why, my friend, I did once hear of someone out in India having a phoenix in his possession, and he had to have three six-headed dragons to guard it day and night, so precious is a phoenix."

"What color would its feathers be?"

"All the colors of the rainbow, so they tell me," replied the old man, "but you understand that I have never seen one."

The merchant thanked him and went into a jeweler's shop and bought a very handsome buckle of pearls and amethysts, and went back home.

His daughter came running to the door.

He fumbled in his pouch and gave her the lovely buckle, and her great gray eyes filled with tears.

"Thank you, Father"—she hardly looked at the jewel—"but where is my feather, a feather of Phoenix the Great Bird?"

"My dear, I searched all over the place for it. And hardly anyone had even heard of such a bird, and then I went to a man who had many falcons to sell, and he told me that Phoenix the Great Bird may not be bought or sold anywhere. It is the rarest of all birds, Child, and the man heard of someone in a remote country having three six-headed dragons to guard a phoenix by day and by night, so precious it is."

"Oh dear," said the girl. "I am so sorry. I did look forward to just one white feather."

"Its feathers are not white," said the merchant. "The man told me they were all the colors of the rainbow."

"The man did not know, Father," she said, stubbornly. "You see, I have now remembered my dream. It is my fate to possess one such feather—or else to die."

The merchant staggered on his feet.

"It is a great sin to speak of such things, my darling"—he spoke gently—"and you must never say that again. It would be dreadful if any of the maids were to overhear you. Whoever heard of anyone's life being dependent on a bird's feather?"

"It is Phoenix the Great Bird's feather," she said sadly, "and I know it must be my fate, and nobody can escape their fate, can they?"

The merchant wept bitterly.

"I have tried to be an upright man all the years of my life, and why should such a calamity now come to my door? I fear I shall never find any such feather, and I could not bear the thought of losing you—except perhaps to a good husband who would take care of you all through your life."

The daughter said nothing, but kissed her father very tenderly and went into her room.

That night the merchant never closed his eyes for a moment. At daybreak he went out, had his horse saddled, and made for another distant city where, as he had once heard, many rare birds might be bought. He never reached that city, however.

By the roadside he saw a middle-aged man in shabby clothes, with a wooden box in his lap. The box was painted blue and silver and looked rather pretty.

The merchant gave the man the time of the day and was just about to ride past when the man called out, "Could you spare a coin, master? I have had no breakfast."

The merchant rather unwillingly halted his horse.

"Why, you don't look much of a beggar even though your clothes seem shabby. Haven't you any money at all?"

"I gave my very last copper to a beggar I met a few minutes ago," said the man, and added, before the merchant had a moment to exclaim at his impudence, "You won't regret it, master. I can give you this little box in exchange."

"You might just as well take it to the market and sell it there," the merchant told him. "That might buy you a loaf of bread."

"A loaf of bread?" cried the shabby man. "Ah, master, truly has it been said that few men see their luck until it has passed them. There is a feather of Phoenix the Great Bird in it."

The merchant leaped out of his saddle as though he had been stung by a wasp.

"I must have it," he cried hoarsely. "Man, I would give you more than one half of my possessions for that feather." And he held out both hands, but the shabby man got up and moved back a little.

"I have no use for your possessions, master," he said coldly. "And you must not ask me any questions, but this much I can tell you: I was waiting for you by the roadside because I knew that you would pass this way to the city, there to find a feather of Phoenix the Great Bird. But you would not have found it in any shop in the world, and I am not going to sell it to you either. I know that your daughter has had to ask for it because such is her fate, and I am going to let you have it on one condition—that you promise most solemnly never to believe any wrong that may be said of her."

"Believe any wrong said of my beloved daughter?" cried the merchant in high indignation. "I should be mad indeed if I ever did such a wicked thing. My daughter has not a single fault in her. Goodness, I would kill anyone who dared whisper anything against her."

"Promise, then," said the stranger, and the merchant swore a terrible oath, and then turned back home, the little painted box safely hidden in his saddlebag.

His daughter was almost speechless for joy when she opened the box and saw the little white feather. She took it upstairs to her room, and as soon as she had touched it, she remembered her dream in all its details, and she knew what she must do. She at once bolted the door and drew the curtains close together. Then she lit the candle, picked up the white feather, and let it fall on the floor. At once a handsome young prince stood in her room and looked at her, and the merchant's daughter looked back at him and then bent her eyes shyly. Both knew they were meant for each other, and the room remained very still for some minutes.

Then the Prince said, "I have been wandering all over the world, my love. I knew you would be beautiful, but I was not looking only for beauty. I was meant to find someone with a soul and a heart as pure and white as the feather into which I return from time to time. Now that I have found you, my quest is over."

She breathed softly.

"You are my fate, my love, my all, but I never knew you would be a prince." Here she bowed to him. "I am but a merchant's daughter."

"You are a princess," he told her fierily, "because I have chosen you."

Here they heard a knock on the door, and instantly the white feather was returned to the box, and the girl hurried to open the door to a maid.

"We thought we heard a noise in your room," said the servant, peering in.

"It was an owl on the window sill," replied the merchant's daughter. "Please don't disturb me again. I am going to bed now."

Again she closed the door and opened the box. On tiptoe she carried the white feather to the window, opened it, and whispered, "Fly away, fly away, my lovely one, my Phoenix the Great Bird, and come back sometime."

Then the merchant's daughter went to bed and dreamed the dream again, and she never knew that downstairs her father's servants were all together in the kitchen and wondering about the murmurs they had heard in their young mistress' room. Among them was her old nurse, who got very angry and accused the maid of having invented it all.

"If the master were to hear of it, he would send you packing this very evening," she told the maid.

The girl hotly defended herself and said, "Let us all wait till tomorrow evening, and if I am proved wrong you can complain to the master and let him send me away."

So next evening, just before the moon rose, the merchant's daughter was alone in her room with the door bolted, the window curtained, and the candle lit. There came a delicate tap on the windowpane. She tiptoed across and opened the window, and in flew—not a white feather, but Phoenix the Great Bird, all snow white and silver, his eyes as blue as sapphires and his chest shining like gold. So beautiful was he that the merchant's daughter held her breath in wonder. He flew in and dropped on the floor, and instantly the Prince was before her.

"My love," he whispered, "listen to me carefully. I shall come for the third time tomorrow evening, and after that I must fly far, far away to a country you have never heard of, and there be burned on a great fire to rise out of the ashes. That done, I shall fly back to you and take you away—to my own kingdom."

The merchant's daughter answered very softly, "You are my fate, my love, my all, but I never knew you would be a prince. I am but a merchant's daughter."

"From this hour on you are a princess because I have chosen you," said the Prince, kissed her, turned into Phoenix the Great Bird, and flew out of the window.

The merchant's daughter waited for another knock on the door, but not a sound came, and she went to bed. She never knew that all the maids and her nurse had been listening.

They crept downstairs very cautiously, and once they got to the kitchen, the nurse said, "That such a shame should happen to this house! The young mistress must be bewitched. She has fallen in love with some changeling. It may well be an owl, but I think it must be that white falcon in the neighbor's orchard. I have always thought there was something odd about that bird."

"What are we to do?" asked someone.

The nurse answered, "You leave it to me."

Next evening she slipped a powder into her young mistress' milk, and as soon as she had drunk it, she felt drowsy and was asleep before she had had the time to bolt her door. The nurse crept in, opened the window, put three sharply bladed knives on the window sill, and closing the window, tiptoed out of the room.

Her young mistress lay held in deep sleep. Presently there came a delicate tap. She never heard it, of course. Then came a moan and a cry, but she slept on, and in the morning she woke up, her thoughts all confused after that heavy sleep. Then everything came back to her, and she sprang out of her bed and ran to open the window, and there she saw the three sharply bladed knives and a few drops of blood on the broad stone sill. She cradled her head in her arms and wept bitterly until the nurse came into the room.

"Your father wishes to see you," she said severely, and the merchant's daughter stared.

"But it is so early," she murmured, "and I have had no breakfast. Please fetch me some milk, nurse."

"Never a bite do you get until your father has seen you," answered the old woman, and left the room abruptly.

So the merchant's daughter refreshed her burning face with cold water, braided her hair, and went downstairs. She could not recognize her father's face. It looked as somber as a November night, and his voice ran harsh.

"Who came to see you last evening and the evening before? Don't lie to me. I know someone did."

"My fate, Father," she told him.

He clenched his fists and his face went even darker. He had wholly forgotten the terrible oath sworn by him on the road to the city, and the oath meant that he would die if he believed any wrong of his daughter.

"You are no daughter of mine," he said hoarsely. "You can leave this house at once and I don't care what happens to you."

Sadly she turned back to the stairs, and she never knew that he would die that same day before the sun set.

In her room she knelt by the window and cried, "Oh, my fate, my love, my all, what have these cruel people done to your shining wings? I'd give my heart's blood to have you back, and I don't know what to do except that I must leave this house at once. They say the world is very big, and I shall search for you in all the corners of it, but shall I ever find you, my love, my all?"

Here she raised her head and saw the falcon from the neighbor's orchard fly toward her.

"Falcon, my sweet white falcon," she murmured to him, "teach me how to find my love."

The falcon perched on the broad stone sill and tilted his head a little.

"You should never have drunk that milk last night," he said, "but I fear that you are so good you just can't imagine other people being wicked. It is your nurse and the maids who carried the tale to your father. They eavesdropped outside the door."

The merchant's daughter held her breath.

"Did they hurt my love very badly?"

"No, the tip of his left wing had a cut, that is all," the falcon told her, "but I am afraid he flew away, his heart broken. He just could not understand why you would not wake up. You see, even Phoenix the Great Bird does not know everything that happens in the world. And he stopped in my orchard for a moment and woke me up, and said you were free to search for him, but he also said that you would wear out six pairs of stout shoes in the search."

"Did he say that I would find him in the end, my sweet falcon?"

The falcon hesitated, and she urged him to tell her the whole truth.

"No, he said nothing about the end of the search. You see, he is very proud, and his pride was hurt last night."

So the merchant's daughter slipped out of the house that same day, and she was never to return there. She called at a shoemaker's and bought six pairs of stout shoes and hid them in her satchel, and she started on her travels.

She went on and on and on, and three of the six pairs were worn out, and at last she reached a country where people kept their front doors opened. She stopped outside one, and the woman of the house welcomed her kindly.

"I have heard of you," she said with pity. "You are looking for Phoenix the Great Bird. Ah, my pretty, the way is long and hard, but I have been told to be of some use to you because you have never complained. Here is a little ball of silver thread and a witch-hazel wand. When you have left the city you will come to a crossroads. Roll the ball a little away from you, and it will show you the way, but remember that—once you have reached the crossroads—you must begin a three days' fast, and you must never part either with the wand or the ball of silver thread."

"Shall I ever come to the end of the search?" asked the girl.

"That I can't tell you at all."

So the merchant's daughter thanked the woman for her gifts and went on. She walked through many a forest and crossed many a mountain ridge, and her fourth pair of stout shoes was utterly worn out. Then she came near a pleasant garden with a stream of pure milk running right through it, and she saw a table laid under a thick-girthed tree. There was fresh fruit and bread and cold meat spread on the snowy cloth, and the girl felt so hungry that she nearly fainted when a plump little woman in a brown cloak called out to her.

"Good morning, my pretty one. Come and breakfast with me. There's plenty for two here."

The girl made a step forward when the witch-hazel wand whispered under her hand, "Eat nothing unless you wish to fall asleep forevermore."

"I'd rather not," the merchant's daughter said faintly, "but thank you very much."

"Then sit you down for a bit. You look rather tired."

The girl felt exhausted, and she sat down on a bench near the table and tried to keep her eyes away from the food. It was perfectly dreadful for her to watch the plump little woman in brown eat cold beef and salad and cheese and bread and apples.

"Are you quite sure you won't have anything?" asked the woman and popped a luscious black grape into her mouth. "I wish you would have a small piece of this cheese. It is so good. It is made of pure cream."

The girl hesitated and all but stretched out her hand when again the witch-hazel wand murmured, "Eat nothing unless you wish to fall asleep forevermore."

"No, thank you. I'd rather not," she said again, and got up, because she felt she simply could not watch the plump woman in brown eat another morsel.

A little farther on the girl heard the witch-hazel wand murmur, "Now turn around, and you'll see what you'll see."

The merchant's daughter turned and saw that where the table had stood was nothing but a pile of smoking green wood. She hurried on as fast as her tired legs would carry her, and presently she came to a field where two red-faced peasants were about to have their dinner. They had just broiled some trout in hot ashes, and the poor girl nearly fainted, so tempting was the smell of the fish.

"Come and share our dinner," they called out to her. "You look as though you need it badly, and there's plenty here."

She stood hesitating, and once again the wand warned her not to touch the food.

"No, thank you," she said politely. "I'd rather not."

"Then sit you down and rest," they said.

This time the girl's torment did not last very long. The two men gobbled their fish as fast as they could.

"Where are you going, my pretty one?" one of them asked her.

She replied, "I am on my way to look for a friend."

"And we take it that you are a stranger in this country?"

"Oh yes!"

"Then most likely you have not heard of something that has just happened in this place. The King caught Phoenix the Great Bird and had him burned in the square of the capital. It is said that a white falcon flew over and gathered up all the ashes and dropped them into the sea far, far away. They all say the King got very angry with Phoenix the Great Bird for its witchery."

"But you are wrong, friend," said the second man. "There was no falcon at all. It was the wind that raised the ashes and had them scattered over the sea."

The merchant's daughter sat very still. She wondered if the magic wand would murmur something, and she waited. She heard a very faint sound.

"They can't hurt you. You may tell them the truth."

"Oh dear, oh dear," she moaned, "why, that's the very friend I am looking for."

"You'd better not go near the city," they told her. "The King might hear about you and have you sent to the stake in your turn. The King won't have anything to do with witchery."

She thanked them and shook her head. She was tired, thirsty and very, very hungry, but she went on and on, and that day she wore out the fifth pair of her stout shoes. She put on the sixth and last pair and said to herself, No wonder they wore out so quickly, seeing that my search must be at an end.

On the third day, the merchant's daughter reached the city. She was going down a street where a family sat outside eating supper in the open air. They invited her to sit down and share their food, but once again warned by the wand, she refused.

Then the woman said suddenly, "What a pretty ball of silver thread you have! Go to the palace, my pretty, and the Queen may buy it."

"It is not for sale," the merchant's daughter said politely, and went on till she reached the square.

There was a great crowd around a huge stake, and they were all shouting, "Why, the ashes must have been brought back! The white falcon must have gathered them up again."

The girl's knees shook under her, but she came closer to the stake and she wept until her heart was wrung, and everybody said, "Of course she must be a witch if she can weep for Phoenix the Great Bird."

And at once they sent word to the palace to tell the King of a strange girl weeping by the stake in the square, and the King ordered her to be burned at once. The soldiers tried to tie her to the stake, but they could do nothing at all until by a mischance she loosened her hold on the little ball of silver thread and the men bound her to the stake.

Her little feet stood on the ashes, and she cried, "Oh, my fate, my love, my all! I have endured hunger and thirst and great weariness for you, and none of it matters, because I truly love you and because I have found you at last." And at that moment the merchant's daughter felt something against her left foot, and she looked down, and there lay a gleaming white wing where the ashes had been. She felt something against her right foot, and she looked down again, and there lay another gleaming white wing. She looked down for the third time, and there was the shining head of Phoenix the Great Bird, with his eyes as blue as sapphires and his crest of pure gold.

The crowd fell back in amazement, and even the soldiers were terrified. Then the wings spread, and up flew Phoenix the Great Bird, and in an instant he pecked at the ropes which bound her to the stake. In another instant she was on his wings and they flew away together, and nobody ever saw them again.

From *Russian Folk and Fairy Tales* by E. M. Almedingen. 1957. New York: G. P. Putnam's Sons, pp. 164-179. Copyright © 1957 by the author.

The Phoenix

The Phoenix Today

Reappearing in art and literature through the centuries, the phoenix reveals itself once again in the modern world.

The immortal bird appears unexpectedly in our daily lives. The figure on the hood of a Pontiac Firebird is an eagle-like phoenix with outspread wings. The bird is remembered in place names from the Phoenix Islands in the Pacific Ocean to Phoenixville, Connecticut, and is a constellation in the southern skies. Hundreds of titles, such as *Japan: The Phoenix of Asia*, *A Phoenix Too Frequent*, and *Flight of the Phoenix* figuratively refer to the rebirth of someone or something. Behind a sports page headline—"Phoenix Suns Rise from the Ashes of NBA Despair"—is the myth nearly as old as civilization itself. The Asian phoenix is a standard figure in the decorative arts and in product packaging. And not surprisingly, the Western phoenix appears more than rarely in modern children's stories and adult fantasy novels.

The phoenix remains true to its own myth.

The Phoenix and the Carpet

E. Nesbit

From The Phoenix and the Carpet *by E. Nesbit (1858-1924). Bored in London lodgings during school holidays, Robert, Anthea, Cyril, and Jane try to generate some excitement by dabbling in magic. On the mantelpiece is an egg they found rolled up in an old carpet. "The Lamb" is their absent baby brother.*

o they traced strange figures on the linoleum, on the part where the hearth-rug had kept it clean. They traced them with chalk that Robert had nicked from the top of the mathematical master's desk at school. You know, of course, that it is stealing to take a new stick of chalk, but it is not wrong to take a broken piece, so long as you only take one. (I do not know the reason of this rule, nor who made it.) And they chanted all the gloomiest songs they could think of. And, of course, nothing happened. So then Anthea said, "I'm sure a magic fire ought to be made of sweet-swelling wood, and have magic gums and essences and things in it."

"I don't know any sweet-smelling wood except cedar," said Robert, "but I've got some ends of cedar-wood lead pencil."

So they burned the ends of lead pencil. And still nothing happened.

"Let's burn some of the eucalyptus oil we have for our colds," said Anthea.

And they did. It certainly smelt very strong. And they burned lumps of camphor out of the big chest. It was very bright, and made a horrid black smoke, which looked very magical. But still nothing happened. Then they got some clean tea-cloths from the dresser drawer in the kitchen, and waved them over the magic chalk-tracings, and sang "The Hymn of the Moravian Nuns of Bethlehem," which is very impressive. And still nothing happened. So they waved more and more wildly, and Robert's tea-cloth caught the golden egg and whisked it off the mantel-piece, and it fell into the fender and rolled under the grate.

"Oh, crikey!" said more than one voice.

And every one instantly fell down flat on its front to look under the grate, and there lay the egg, glowing in a nest of hot ashes.

"It's not smashed, anyhow," said Robert, and he put his hand under the grate and picked up the egg. But the egg was much hotter than any one would have believed it could possibly get in such a short time, and Robert had to drop it with a cry of "Bother!" It fell on the top bar of the grate, and bounced right into the glowing red-hot heart of the fire.

"The tongs!" cried Anthea. But alas, no one could remember where they were. Every one had forgotten that the tongs had last been used to fish up the doll's tea-pot from the bottom of the water-butt, where the Lamb had dropped it. So the nursery tongs were resting between the water-butt and the dustbin, and cook refused to lend the kitchen ones.

"Never mind," said Robert, "we'll get it out with the poker and the shovel."

"Oh, stop," cried Anthea. "Look at it! Look! look! look! I do believe something *is* going to happen!"

For the egg was now red-hot, and inside it something was moving. Next moment there was a soft cracking sound; the egg burst in two, and out of it came a flame-coloured bird. It rested a moment among the flames, and as it rested there the four children could see it growing bigger and bigger under their eyes.

Every mouth was a-gape, every eye a-goggle.

The bird rose in its nest of fire, stretched its wings, and flew out into the room. It flew round and round, and round again, and where it passed the air was warm. Then it perched on the fender. The children looked at each other. Then Cyril put out a hand towards the bird. It put its head on one side and looked up at him, as you may have seen a parrot do when it is just going to speak, so that the children were hardly astonished at all when it said, "Be careful; I am not nearly cool yet."

They were not astonished, but they were very, very much interested.

They looked at the bird, and it was certainly worth looking at. Its feathers were like gold. It was about as large as a bantam, only its beak was not at all bantam-shaped.

"I believe I know what it is," said Robert. "I've seen a picture——"

He hurried away. A hasty dash and scramble among the papers on father's study table yielded, as the sum-books say, "the desired result." But when he came back into the room holding out a paper, and crying, "I say, look here," the others all said "Hush!" and he hushed obediently and instantly, for the bird was speaking.

"Which of you," it was saying, "put the egg into the fire?"

"He did," said three voices, and three fingers pointed at Robert.

The bird bowed; at least it was more like that than anything else.

"I am your grateful debtor," it said with a high-bred air.

The children were all choking with wonder and curiosity—all except Robert. He held the paper in his hand, and he *knew*. He said so. He said:

"*I* know who you are."

And he opened and displayed a printed paper, at the head of which was a little picture of a bird sitting in a nest of flames.

"You are the Phoenix," said Robert; and the bird was quite pleased.

"My fame has lived then for two thousand years," it said. "Allow me to look at my portrait."

It looked at the page which Robert, kneeling down, spread out on the fender, and said:

"It's not a flattering likeness. . . . And what are these characters?" it asked, pointing to the printed part.

"Oh, that's all dullish; it's not much about you, you know," said Cyril, with unconscious politeness; "but you're in lots of books——"

"With portraits?" asked the Phoenix.

"Well, no," said Cyril; "in fact, I don't think I ever saw any portrait of you but that one, but I can read you something about yourself, if you like."

The Phoenix nodded, and Cyril went off and fetched Volume X. of the old Encyclopaedia, and on page 246 he found the following:

"Phoenix—in ornithology, a fabulous bird of antiquity."

"Antiquity is quite correct," said the Phoenix, "but fabulous—well, do I look it?"

Every one shook its head. Cyril went on: "The ancients speak of this bird as single, or the only one of its kind."

"That's right enough," said the Phoenix.

"They describe it as about the size of an eagle."

"Eagles are of different sizes," said the Phoenix; "it's not at all a good description."

All the children were kneeling on the hearthrug, to be as near the Phoenix as possible.

"You'll boil your brains," it said. "Look out, I'm nearly cool now"; and with a whirr of golden wings it fluttered from the fender to the table. It was so nearly cool that there was only a very faint smell of burning when it had settled itself on the table-cloth.

"It's only a very little scorched," said the Phoenix, apologetically; "it will come out in the wash. Please go on reading."

The children gathered round the table.

"The size of an eagle," Cyril went on, "its head finely crested with a beautiful plumage, its neck covered with feathers of a gold colour, and the rest of its body purple; only the tail white, and the eyes sparkling like stars. They say that it lives about five hundred years in the wilderness, and when advanced in age it builds itself a pile of sweet wood and aromatic gums, fires it with the wafting of its wings, and thus burns itself; and that from its ashes arises a worm, which in time grows up to be a Phoenix. Hence the Phoenicians gave——"

"Never mind what they gave," said the Phoenix, ruffling its golden feathers. "They never gave much, anyway; they always were people who gave nothing for nothing. That book ought to be destroyed. It's most inaccurate. The rest of my body was *never* purple, and as for my tail—well, I simply ask you, *is* it white?"

It turned round and gravely presented its golden tail to the children.

"No, it's not," said everybody.

"No, and it never was," said the Phoenix. "And that about the worm is just a vulgar insult. The Phoenix has an egg, like all respectable birds. It makes a pile—that part's all right—and it lays its egg, and it burns itself; and it goes to sleep and wakes up in its egg, and comes out and goes on living again, and so on for ever and ever. I can't tell you how weary I got of it—such a restless existence; no repose."

"But how did your egg get *here*?" asked Anthea.

"Ah, that's my life-secret," said the Phoenix. "I couldn't tell it to any one who wasn't really sympathetic. I've always been a misunderstood bird. You can tell that by what they say about the worm. I might tell *you*," it went on, looking at Robert with eyes that were indeed starry. "*You* put me on the fire——"

Robert looked uncomfortable.

"The rest of us made the fire of sweet-scented woods and gums, though," said Cyril.

"And—and it was an accident my putting you on the fire," said Robert, telling the truth with some difficulty, for he did not know how the Phoenix might take it. It took it in the most unexpected manner.

"Your candid avowal," it said, "removes my last scruple. I will tell you my story."

"And you won't vanish, or anything sudden, will you?" asked Anthea, anxiously.

"Why?" it asked, puffing out the golden feathers, "do you wish me to stay here?"

"Oh, *yes*," said every one, with unmistakable sincerity.

"Why?" asked the Phoenix again, looking modestly at the table-cloth.

"Because," said every one at once, and then stopped short; only Jane added after a pause, "you are the most beautiful person we've ever seen."

"You are a sensible child," said the Phoenix, "and I will *not* vanish or anything sudden. And I will tell you my tale. I had resided, as your book says, for many thousand years in the wilderness, which is a larger, quiet place with very little really good society, and I was becoming weary of the monotony of my existence. But I had acquired the habit of laying my egg and burning myself every five hundred years—and you know how difficult it is to break yourself of a habit."

"Yes," said Cyril. "Jane used to bite her nails."

"But I broke myself of it," urged Jane, rather hurt, "you know I did."

"Not till they put bitter aloes on them," said Cyril.

"I doubt," said the bird, gravely, "whether even bitter aloes (the aloe, by the way, has a bad habit of its own, which it might well cure before seeking to cure others; I allude to its indolent practice of flowering but once a century), I doubt whether even bitter aloes could have cured *me*. But I *was* cured. I awoke one morning from a feverish dream—it was getting near the time for me to lay that tiresome fire and lay that tedious egg upon it—and I saw two people, a man and a woman. They were sitting on a carpet—and when I accosted them civilly they narrated to me their life-story, which, as you have not yet heard it, I will now proceed to relate. They were a prince and princess, and the story of their parents was one which I am sure you will like to hear. In early youth the mother of the princess happened to hear the story of a certain enchanter, and in that story, I am sure you will be interested. The enchanter——"

"Oh, please don't," said Anthea. "I can't understand all these beginnings of stories, and you seem to be getting deeper and deeper in them every minute. Do tell us your *own* story. That's what we really want to hear."

"Well," said the Phoenix, seeming on the whole rather flattered, "to cut about seventy long stories short (though *I* had to listen to them all—but to be sure in the wilderness there is plenty of time), this prince and princess were so fond of each other that they did not want any one else, and the enchanter—don't be alarmed, I won't go into his history—had given them a magic carpet (you've heard of a magic carpet?), and they had just sat on it and told it to take them right away from every one—and it had brought them to the wilderness. And as they meant to stay there they had no further use for the carpet, so they gave it to me. That was indeed the chance of a life-time!"

"I don't see what you wanted with a carpet," said Jane, "when you've got those lovely wings."

"They *are* nice wings, aren't they?" said the Phoenix, simpering and spreading them out. "Well, I got the prince to lay out the carpet, and I laid my egg on it; then I said to the carpet, 'Now, my excellent carpet, prove your worth. Take that egg somewhere where it can't be hatched for two thousand years, and where, when that time's up, some one will light a fire of sweet wood and aromatic gums, and put the egg in to hatch'; and you see it's all come out exactly as I said. The words were no sooner out of my beak than egg and carpet disappeared. The royal lovers assisted to arrange my pile, and soothed my last moments. I burnt myself up, and knew no more till I awoke on yonder altar."

It pointed its claw at the grate.

"But the carpet," said Robert, "the magic carpet that takes you anywhere you wish. What became of that?"

"Oh, *that*?" said the Phoenix, carelessly—"I should say that that *is* the carpet. I remember the pattern perfectly."

It pointed as it spoke to the floor, where lay the carpet which mother had bought in the Kentish Town Road for twenty-two shillings and ninepence.

From *The Phoenix and the Carpet* by E. Nesbit. Reprint, London: Octopus Books, 1979, pp. 197-205.

David and the Phoenix

Edward Ormondroyd

In Edward Ormondroyd's David and the Phoenix *(1958), a boy hiking behind his family's new home discovers a large talking bird. After a series of fantastic adventures, with "the Scientist" in pursuit of the rare phoenix, David meets his bizarre friend up in the mountains for a special birthday celebration. As the bird had requested, David gives him a present of cinnamon, and the phoenix reveals its timeless nature.*

 t last the ice cream carton was empty and all the cookies were gone. They both sighed regretfully and brushed away the crumbs. And the Phoenix looked hopefully at the present David had brought.

"Happy birthday, Phoenix," David said, and he handed the gift over with a little bow.

"Thank you, my boy, thank you." The Phoenix opened the package eagerly and gave a pleased cry. "*Just* what I wanted, my dear chap!"

"I'm glad you like it," David said. "Do you know yet what it's for? Can you really use it for something?"

The Phoenix suddenly stopped smiling and looked at David with a strange expression on its face—an expression David had never seen there before. A vague dread swept through him, and he faltered, "Phoenix . . . you *do* know what it's for? What is it? Tell me."

"Well, my boy—well, the fact *is*—yes, I do know. It came to me this morning while I was constructing the—ah—nest, here. I am afraid it will be a bit hard to explain. The cinnamon—ah—the cinnamon—well, cinnamon *branches* are what I should really have . . ."

"But Phoenix, what's it *for*?"

"Behold, my boy." The Phoenix opened the boxes, and spread the cinnamon sticks on the nest. Then it took the cans and sprinkled the cinnamon powder over the top and sides of the heap, until the whole nest was a brick-dust red.

"There we are, my boy," said the Phoenix sadly. "The traditional cinnamon pyre of the Phoenix, celebrated in song and story."

And with the third mention of the word "pyre," David's legs went weak and something seemed to catch in his throat. He remembered now where he had heard that word before. It was in his book of explorers, and it meant—it meant—

"Phoenix," he choked, "wh-wh-who is the pyre for?"

"For myself," said the Phoenix.

"Phoenix!"

"Now, I implore you—please—oh, dear, I *knew* it would be difficult to explain. Look at me, my boy."

David did as he was told, although his eyes were filled with tears and he could not see through the blur.

"Now," said the Phoenix gently, "the fact is that I have, besides my unusually acute Intellect, an Instinct. This Instinct told me that it was my birthday today. It also told me to build this nest of cinnamon. Now it tells me that I must make this nest my pyre, because that is what the Phoenix does at the end of five hundred years. Now, please, my boy!—I admit it does not appear to be a very joyful way of celebrating, but it must be done. This is the traditional end of the Phoenix, my boy, and we cannot ignore the tradition, no matter what our feelings may be. Do you see?"

"No!" David cried. "Please, Phoenix, don't do it! It's horrible! I won't let you do it!"

"But I must, my dear chap! I cannot help it. This is what it means to be the Phoenix. Nothing can stop the tradition. Please, my boy, do not take on so! It is not in the least horrible, I assure you. My Instinct tells me so."

"You said you were going to give me an education," David sobbed. "You said we would see—you said—and we've only been on four adventures—you never told me about this—"

"I'm terribly sorry, my boy. I could not tell you about it because I did not *know* about it until now. As for your education, it is a pity to have it cut short in this way. I had great plans . . . But consider—you have had four adventures which no one else in the whole world has had! And besides, my boy, we shall see each other again. I do not know how or where, but I am positive of it." The Phoenix flicked a tear from its eye with the tip of one wing, while with the other it patted David awkwardly on the shoulder.

"Don't go, Phoenix, *please* don't go."

"I must, my boy. Here, permit me to present you with a small token (ouch!) of our friendship."

Dimly, through his tears, David saw the Phoenix pluck the longest, bluest feather from its tail, and he felt it being pressed into his hand.

"Good-bye, David," said the Phoenix gruffly.

David could stand it no longer. He turned and rushed blindly from the Phoenix, blundered into the thicket, and dropped to the ground with his head buried in his arms. Behind him he heard the sticks snapping as the Phoenix mounted its pyre. A match rasped against the box. The first tongue of flame sizzled in the branches. David pressed his hands over his ears to shut out the sound, but he could feel the heat of the flames as they sprang up. And the noise would not be shut out. It grew and grew, popping, crackling, roaring, until it seemed to fill the world . . .

* * *

Perhaps he fainted. Or perhaps from numbness he slipped into a kind of deep sleep. Whichever it was, he returned to consciousness again suddenly. His hands had slipped from his ears, and a sound had brought him back. He lifted his head and listened. The fire had burnt itself out now. The only noise was the hiss and pop of dying embers. But these sounds were too gentle to have awakened him—it must have been something else. Yes—it was a voice. He could hear it quite plainly now. There were angry shouts coming from somewhere below the ledge.

Carefully avoiding the sight of the pyre, David crawled to the edge and glanced over. Far down, on the slope at the foot of the scarp, was a tiny figure dancing and bellowing with rage. The Scientist had returned and discovered the ruins of his blind. David watched him dully. No need to worry about him any more. How harmless he looked now, even ridiculous! David turned away.

He noticed then that he was holding something in his hand, something soft and heavy. As he lifted it to look more closely, it flashed in the sunlight. It was the feather the Phoenix had given him, the tail feather. Tail feather? . . . but the Phoenix's tail had been a sapphire blue. The feather in his hand was of the purest, palest gold.

There was a slight stir behind him. In spite of himself, he glanced at the remains of the pyre. His mouth dropped open. In the middle of the white ashes and glowing coals there was movement. Something within was struggling up toward the top. The noises grew stronger and more definite. Charred sticks were being snapped, ashes kicked aside, embers pushed out of the way. Now, like a plant thrusting its way out of the soil, there appeared something pale and glittering, which nodded in the breeze. Little tongues of flame, it seemed, licking out into the air . . . No, not flames! A crest of golden feathers! . . . A heave from below lifted the ashes in the center of the pile, a fine cloud of flakes swirled up into the breeze, there was a flash of sunlight glinting on brilliant plumage. And from the ruins of the pyre stepped forth a magnificent bird.

It was the Phoenix, it must be the Phoenix! But it was a new and different Phoenix. It was young and wild, with a fierce amber eye; its crest was tall and proud, its body the slim, muscular body of a hunter, its wings narrow and long and pointed like a falcon's, the great beak and talons razor-sharp and curving. And all of it, from crest to talons, was a burnished gold that reflected the sun in a thousand dazzling lights.

The bird stretched its wings, shook the ash from its tail, and began to preen itself. Every movement was like the flash of a silent explosion.

"Phoenix," David whispered. "Phoenix."

* * *

The bird, with one clear, defiant cry, leaped to an outjutting boulder. The golden wings spread, the golden neck curved back, the golden talons pushed against the rock. The bird launched itself into the air and soared out over the valley, sparkling, flashing, shimmering; a flame, large as a sunburst, a meteor, a diamond, a star, diminishing at last to a speck of gold dust, which glimmered twice in the distance before it was gone altogether.

From *David and the Phoenix* by Edward Ormondroyd. Chicago: Follett Publishing, 1958, pp. 165-173. Copyright © 1957 by Edward Ormondroyd.

The Phoenix

The Griffin

The Griffin

ost majestic of all the beasts of the imagination, the griffin is a fusion of the two mightiest animals of earth and sky—the lion and the eagle. Over the centuries and from one land to another, this wonder beast has taken on so many shapes and characteristics that it is often difficult to recognize.

This master of two worlds has been the vigilant guardian of treasure and of kings. It has pulled the chariots of Pharaoh, Apollo, Nemesis, and Alexander the Great. A major heraldic animal, it has been emblazoned on the shields of knights and on the coats of arms of royalty. It has been watchful and loyal, graceful and swift, rapacious and vengeful, monstrous and divine. While the griffin is a mortal enemy of horses, its magic talons have detected poison and its feathers have cured blindness.

It has had the forefeet of a lion or a bird of prey and the body of a lion, panther, or dog. On its head, it has worn a decorative knob, ram's horns, crests, crowns, and ringlets. Winged lions are not true griffins, nor is the winged lion of the sea, with a serpent's tail, nor the Dragon of Wales, with its reptilian wings. All of them, though—along with countless other hybrid variations—are "gryphonic."

Once you recognize the basic eagle-lion shape of the powerful beast, you will see it all around you: on business signs and coats of arms, in paint, stone, metal, wood, and stained glass.

The Griffin from the Past

The griffin is one of the oldest and grandest of fabulous animals. Like other wonder beasts, its appearance and its stories change from age to age, reflecting the values and beliefs of different societies.

"Griffin" (griffon, gryphon, gryffon, etc.) comes from the Greek word *gryps*, meaning "curled, curved, having a hooked nose." The griffon-vulture is of the genus *Gyps*. The griffin and the eagle have shared a constellation with the phoenix.

Griffins of the Ancients

A 5,000-year-old figure with the head and front feet of a bird of prey and the body of a lion walks on a cylinder seal from the ancient city of Susa, in what is now Iran. Other early forms of the griffin appeared in Egyptian tomb paintings and Mesopotamian cylinder seals.

Susa griffin. (Sketch by Esther Muzzillo. From *The Evolution of the Dragon* by G. Elliot Smith.)

Graceful Cretan griffins protected kings and drew the chariots of goddesses. In the restored Palace of Minos, at Knossos, painted griffins with peacock crests guard the royal throne. The beast becomes more fierce in Greek art. Bronze griffin heads, with the decorative knob, feature a hooked beak, pointed ears and tongue. In Greek vase paintings, the griffin is often depicted attacking other animals or men, but the beast was also associated with the god Apollo and the goddesses Athena and Nemesis.

Cretan griffin.

A common ornamental figure in ancient art, the griffin made only brief appearances in early literature. In the best-known ancient story about griffins, the creatures guard gold up in wild, distant mountains and wage constant warfare with the one-eyed Arimaspi and others who would steal their treasure. An account of the tale, Herodotus said, was in an epic poem, *The Arimaspeia*, written by Aristeas of Proconnesus. Both Pliny and Aelian also recount the story of the gold-guarding griffins.

In his book on the wonders of India, Ctesias, a Greek physician to the Persian court, describes the griffin as a four-footed bird as large as a wolf, with legs and claws like a lion's. This beast, he said, is covered with black feathers except for red feathers on its breast.

The Medieval Griffin

The griffin was a complex animal during the Middle Ages. It was treated as both an agent of the Devil and as a beast of God.

The bestiaries present the griffin as a violent, evil animal that attacks horses and tears human beings to pieces. Bestiary illustrations show the griffin gripping pigs and other animals in its claws. In Christian sculpture, the griffin is often a monster that devours sinners.

A griffin envoy of the Devil snatches a king's son from a feasting hall in the German epic, *Gudrun*. The boy, Hagan, escapes to a cave where he finds three princesses who had also been abducted by the griffins but had eluded them. One day Hagan finds a dead knight washed up on the seashore, dons his armor, kills the griffins, and leads the maidens to safety.

In another story, griffins pluck sailors from ships and carry them back to their nests to feast upon them. Rabbi Benjamin of Tudela heard a version of the tale during his travels to the Far East. Prester John, the fictional Emperor of India, wrote that in his kingdom were great gryffon birds that carried horses and oxen to their nests. And in his *Travels*, Sir John Mandeville celebrates the strength of the rapacious beasts.

But the griffin also had a more positive role in medieval symbolism. Church fathers made the lion-eagle griffin a symbol of the earthly and divine natures of Christ, and in Dante's *Divine Comedy*, the griffin pulls the chariot of the Church. The iconography of St. Mark as a winged lion is very griffin-like.

In St. Mark's Church in Venice there is a scene from one of the most popular stories of the Middle Ages. Alexander the Great, looking for new worlds to conquer, wanted to journey into the sky. He built a chariot and harnessed griffins to it. Then he stuck meat on spears and held the meat above the beasts' heads. To reach the food, the griffins began to flap their wings. The meat ever out of their reach, the flying animals carried Alexander up into the sky. The griffin is sometimes pictured on Alexander's shield.

The Heraldic Griffin

Long associated with rulers of both the earth and the sky, the majestic griffin was a natural choice as an heraldic beast. The griffin is among the most celebrated animals in heraldry. The sharp ears of the griffin distinguish it from the head of the heraldic eagle. In heraldry, only the female griffin has wings; the male often has spikes spreading from its shoulders like rays of light. The opinicus, with lion forefeet and a short tail like a camel, is a close heraldic relative of the griffin. The griffin is commonly depicted on the shields and helmets of knights in Hollywood movies.

The Griffin Challenged

Heraldic griffin.

The seventeenth-century English writer, Sir Thomas Browne, rejected traditional griffin lore in his *Vulgar Errors* (1646), as he denied ancient stories about the phoenix, the unicorn, and other animals we now regard as fabulous. The griffin, Browne wrote, is not an actual animal but a figure symbolizing the admirable qualities of a guardian. Also, he said, the beast is:

An Emblem of valour and magnanimity, as being compounded of the Eagle and the Lion, the noblest animals in their kinds; and so it is applicable unto Princes, Presidents, Generals, and all heroic Commanders, and so it is also borne in the Coat of Arms of many noble Families of Europe.

Heraldic griffins.

Griffin. (Albrecht Dürer.)

Alexander Ross defended the griffin against Browne's charges:

If any man say that there are now no such animals to be seen, I answer that that may be so, but simply because they are not seen does not mean they do not exist or that they have perished, for maybe they have moved to places that are more remote and safer because they are inaccessible to men.

Once again, though, Ross's defense was no match for the New Science. Artistic and heraldic images of the griffin remained, but like the other wonder beasts, the literary griffin faded from the world for a time.

The Gold-Guarding Griffins

Herodotus

Herodotus wrote in his History *that in a lost epic poem, the poet Aristeas said he traveled as far north as the Issedones. Above them lived the one-eyed Arimaspi, above them the eagle-lion griffins, and above them—stretching right up to the sea—was the land of the Hyperboreans. From the fifth century B.C., this is one of the earliest griffin references.*

he northern parts of Europe are very much richer in gold than any other region: but how it is procured I have no certain knowledge. The story runs, that the one-eyed Arimaspi purloin it from the griffins; but here too I am incredulous, and cannot persuade myself that there is a race of men born with one eye, who in all else resemble the rest of mankind. Nevertheless it seems to be true that the extreme regions of the earth, which surround and shut up within themselves all other countries, produce the things which are the rarest, and which men reckon the most beautiful.

From *The History of Herodotus*, translated by George Rawlinson. New York: D. Appleton, 1859.

The Griffins and the One-Eyed Arimaspi

Pliny the Elder

Five hundred years after Herodotus, in the first century A.D., the Roman Pliny took up the classical tale of the griffins defending their treasure against the one-eyed Arimaspians. Scythia was the ancient name for the area north and northeast of the Black Sea. In Homer's Odyssey, *Odysseus encounters both the Cyclops, one-eyed giants, and the giant cannibals.*

e have pointed out that some Scythian tribes, and in fact a good many, feed on human bodies—a statement that perhaps may seem incredible if we do not reflect that races of this portentous character have existed in the central region of the world, named Cyclopes and Laestrygones, and that quite recently the tribes of the parts beyond the Alps habitually practised human sacrifice, which is not far removed from eating human flesh. But also a tribe is reported next to these, towards the North, not far from the actual quarter whence the North Wind rises and the cave that bears its name, the place called the Earth's Doorbolt—the Arimaspi whom we have spoken of already, people remarkable for having one eye in the centre of the forehead. Many authorities, the most distinguished being Herodotus and Aristeas of Proconnesus, write that these people wage continual war around their mines with the griffins, a kind of wild beast with wings, as commonly reported, that digs gold out of mines, which the creatures guard and the Arimaspi try to take from them, both with remarkable covetousness.

From *Natural History*, Volume III, by Pliny the Elder. Translated by H. Rackham, Cambridge, Mass.: Harvard University Press, 1983, p. 513.

The Gryphons of India

Aelian

By the time the griffins make it into On the Characteristics of
Animals, *an entertaining book of animal lore written by the Roman
Aelian [EH-lee-an], about A.D. 170-235, the eagle-lion beasts have
moved to India. An exotic land to the east, India was so renowned for its
riches that even its sands were said to be of gold. These Indian griffins,
though, still guard gold, and men still try to steal it from them. Aelian
offers his readers the most dramatic griffin story of any of the ancient
writers.*

have heard that the Indian animal the Gryphon is a quad-
ruped like a lion; that it has claws of enormous strength
and that they resemble those of a lion. Men commonly
report that it is winged and that the feathers along its back
are black, and those on its front are red, while the actual
wings are neither but are white. And Ctesias records that its neck is
variegated with feathers of a dark blue; that it has a beak like an eagle's,
and a head too, just as artists portray it in pictures and sculpture. Its
eyes, he says, are like fire. It builds its lair among the mountains, and
although it is not possible to capture the full-grown animal, they do
take the young ones. And the people of Bactria, who are neighbours of
the Indians, say that the Gryphons guard the gold in those parts; that
they dig it up and build their nests with it, and that the Indians carry
off any that falls from them. The Indians however deny that they guard
the aforesaid gold, for the Gryphons have no need of it (and if that is
what they say, then I at any rate think that they speak the truth), but
that they themselves come to collect the gold, while the Gryphons
fearing for their young ones fight with the invaders. They engage too
with other beasts and overcome them without difficulty, but they will
not face the lion or the elephant. Accordingly the natives, dreading the
strength of these animals, do not set out in quest of the gold by day,
but arrive by night, for at that season they are less likely to be detected.
Now the region where the Gryphons live and where the gold is mined
is a dreary wilderness. And the seekers after the aforesaid substance
arrive, a thousand or two strong, armed and bringing spades and sacks;
and watching for a moonless night they begin to dig. Now if they
contrive to elude the Gryphons they reap a double advantage, for they

not only escape with their lives but they also take home their freight, and when those who have acquired a special skill in the smelting of gold have refined it, they possess immense wealth to requite them for the dangers described above. If however they are caught in the act, they are lost. And they return home, I am told, after an interval of three or four years.

From *On the Characteristics of Animals*, Volume I, by Aelian, translated by A. F. Scholfield. Cambridge, Mass.: Harvard University Press, 1971, pp. 241, 243. Copyright by the President and Fellows of Harvard College, 1958.

Griffins of the China Seas

Benjamin of Tudela

In the twelfth century, a hundred years before Marco Polo, Rabbi Benjamin of Tudela was one of the very first Europeans—if not the first—to mention China, which he called Zin. In this tale from The Itinerary of Benjamin of Tudela, *the Rabbi repeats a story he heard during his wanderings.*

hence to cross over to the land of Zin is a voyage of forty days. Zin is in the uttermost East, and some say that there is the Sea of Nikpa, where the star Orion predominates and stormy winds prevail. At times the helmsman cannot govern his ship, as a fierce wind drives her into this Sea of Nikpa, where she cannot move from her place; and the crew have to remain where they are till their stores of food are exhausted and then they die. In this way many a ship has been lost, but men eventually discovered a device by which to escape from this evil place. The crew provide themselves with hides of oxen. And when this evil wind blows which drives them into the Sea of Nikpa, they wrap themselves up in the skins, which they make waterproof, and, armed with knives, plunge into the sea. A great bird called the griffin spies them out, and in the belief that the sailor is an animal, the griffin seizes hold of him, brings him to dry land, and puts him down on a mountain or in a hollow in order to devour him. The man then quickly thrusts at the bird with a knife and slays him. Then the man issues forth from the skin and walks till he comes to an inhabited place. And in this manner many a man escapes.

From *The Itinerary of Benjamin of Tudela*, by Benjamin of Tudela. New York: Philipp Feldheim, n.d., p. 66.

The Griffons of Bactria

Sir John Mandeville

Sir John Mandeville's famous Travels *(circa 1371) is now regarded as a skillful collection of tall-tale material from many sources, including books of the ancient writers. His description of the griffins of Bactria is one of the best-known accounts of that beast. Bactria was an ancient country in Western Asia.*

rom this land men go to the land of Bactria, where there are many wicked and cruel men. In this land there are trees that bear wool, like that of sheep, from which they make cloth. In this land too there are many hippopotami, which live sometimes on dry land and sometimes in the water; they are half man and half horse. And they eat men, whenever they can get them, no meat more readily. And in that land are many griffons, more than in any other country. Some men say they have the foreparts of an eagle and the hindparts of a lion; that is indeed true. Nevertheless the griffon is bigger and stronger than eight lions of these countries, and bigger and stronger than a hundred eagles. For certainly he will carry to his nest in flight a great horse with a man on his back, or two oxen yoked together, as they work together at the plough. He has talons on his feet as great and as long as the horns of oxen, and they are very sharp. Of these talons men make cups to drink out of, as we do with the horns of bulls; and the ribs of his feathers they make into strong bows to shoot with.

From the land of Bactria men go many days' journey to the land of Prester John, who is Emperor of India; and his land is called the isle of Pentoxere.

From *The Travels of Sir John Mandeville*. New York: The Macmillan Company, 1905, p. 177.

The Griffin Around the World

The griffin is one of the many fabulous creatures scholars call *Wundervogel*, "wonder birds." These gigantic fowl are so large they blot out the sun in their flight, casting shadows as large as clouds, and they are so strong they can carry off elephants and oxen. Many of them are enemies of snakes.

Some writers point out that these wonder birds may have derived from great birds like the condor, bones of pterodactyls, or natural phenomena such as mirages, waterspouts, typhoons, and tornadoes.

The Rukh

During his travels, Marco Polo heard about "the gryphon birds" of Madagascar. But these birds, he wrote, were not the same as the bird and lion beasts his kinsmen knew as gryphons. The creatures of Madagascar, which the natives called rukhs, were birds with a wingspan of anywhere from sixteen to thirty paces (forty to seventy-five feet) and feathers eight to twelve paces long (about twenty to thirty feet). Kublai Khan, the Emperor of China, supposedly heard about the giant birds and sent an envoy to Madagascar to verify the story. The envoy, it was said, returned to the Khan with a gigantic rukh feather, delighting the emperor. These rukhs, the natives said, were so large they would prey on elephants. The birds would snatch the gentle beasts in their talons, lift them into the sky, drop them, and feed on them.

Another actual traveler who encountered stories of the rukh was the Arabian, Ibn Battuta, who was born circa 1300, right about the time Marco Polo's travels were written down. Battuta wrote in his *Travels* that while sailing in the China Seas, the crew spotted what they at first thought was a mountain. The mountain, though, was not on any chart, and the next morning the crew thought it had risen above the sea. They began to weep, certain that what they saw was the dreaded rukh, approaching to gobble them up. A fresh wind arose, carrying the ship safely off in another direction, leaving whatever it was behind them.

The rukh. (Illustration by Edward Lane.)

Other travelers told of a bird in the Indian Seas that could carry off a ship in its beak. Natives, some said, cut off the beaks of gigantic dead birds and used them as boats.

The most famous rukh (roc) story of them all is Sindbad's tale in *The Arabian Nights*. Abandoned on an island by his shipmates, Sindbad discovers a white dome that turns out to be an egg of the monstrous roc. To escape the island, Sindbad uses his turban to tie himself to a talon of the nesting bird. When the roc flies off in search of food the next morning, it carries Sindbad over the sea to his next adventure. On a later voyage, the other merchants kill and roast a roc chick and the avenging parents drop boulders onto the departing ship. Sindbad saves himself by clinging to a plank of the sinking vessel.

Bones and fossilized eggs of an actual gigantic bird have been discovered on the island of Madagascar, leading some scholars to believe that the extinct *Aepyornis maximus* was a model for the fabulous rukh. The ostrich-like bird was believed to be about sixteen feet tall. One of its eggs, now displayed in the British Museum, measures 9½ x 13 inches.

The Hippogryph

The closest relative of the griffin is a hybrid called the hippogryph ("hippo," meaning "horse," plus griffin). Traditionally, the griffin was the mortal enemy of the horse, but ancient artists combined the two in the figure of the hippogryph. Later, the hero of Ariosto's Renaissance epic, *Orlando Furioso*, rides the wonderful creature with a magic bridle, much like the Greek hero Bellerophon rode the winged horse Pegasus.

The Simurgh

The wise old Persian Bird of Ages, sometimes called the Senmurv, or Dog-bird, had the powers of reason and human speech. It was said to nest in the Tree of Knowledge and that the wind caused by its flight to and from the nest spread the seeds of wisdom all over the earth.

In the Persian epic, *The Shah Nameh* by Firdausi, the Simurgh finds Zal, a boy abandoned on a mountain by his warrior father. The Simurgh raises Zal and gives him a magic feather when the boy is old enough to return to the world. Years later, when his wife Rudabah is dying in childbirth, Zal calls upon the power of the feather and Rudabah gives birth to the great Persian hero, Rustam.

Hippogryph.

The Anka

This Arabian bird, with a lifespan of 1,700 years, lived on the mountain of Damaj until it carried off a human child and Allah banished it to remote peaks behind the veils of Light and Darkness. A prophet found the child and returned it to its mother.

The Hatthilinga

A fabled gigantic bird of Burma, the Hatthilinga, too, carried off a human being. Its prey, though, was a pregnant Queen, who fell from the bird's grasp onto a mountainside. She gave birth to a son who later gave her brooch to a mountain man in exchange for the freedom of a beautiful snake. The brooch eventually came to the attention of the King, who led his armies to the mountain and returned to the city in triumph with his wife and son.

Garuda

A gigantic man-bird with a white face, scarlet wings, and golden body, Garuda appears in the epics of India, the *Mahabharata* and the *Ramayana*. Brighter than the sun, he carries the god Vishnu through the heavens. He stole the elixir of the gods and once brought two heroes back to life with the touch of his wing.

Garuda.

Thunderbird

In mythologies around the world, the forces of the sky—clouds, wind, rain, thunder, and lightning—are commonly personified by birds. Thunderbird is one of the most widespread of these figures, appearing in myths of Native American tribes across North and South America. Thunderbird shakes the air with his wings and shoots arrows of lightning out of the clouds.

In some tales, Thunderbird wears a garment of eagle skin and a snake belt, which he snaps like a whip, splitting the sky with white fire. To some plains tribes, he was the enemy of water snakes, and to tribes of the Northwest, he was enemy of the whale, carrying the beast high into stormy air and dropping it, shaking the sea. The emblematic American eagle, depicted on a one-dollar bill with arrows in its claws, is a modern descendant of Thunderbird.

Oshadega

The Great Dew Eagle of the Iroquois, Oshadega is a close relative of Thunderbird. It lives in the sky with Hino the Thunderer; his wife, Rainbow; and the Lesser Thunderers. Oshadega carries a lake on its back, and when it flaps its wings, the water splashes into the sky, raining down upon the earth.

Raven

This creator and trickster is a major figure in the tales of the Native Americans of the Northwest. Alive before he was born, Raven created the world, drew human beings out of clamshells, and stole water from the spring of Old Kannuk and spread it over the earth. By trickery, he made off with the bright ball of the sun hidden in the house of a chief, providing sunlight to human beings. He stole salmon from Beaver and dropped pairs of the fish into rivers and lakes. He even moved Beaver's lake by rolling it up and carrying it to another place. Raven never ages. It is said there are so many stories of Raven that it would take a lifetime to tell them all.

The Griffin in Folklore

The talons that could rip the griffin's prey to pieces could also serve humans. According to medieval legend, the claws of the griffin, like the unicorn's horn, had medicinal powers. A drinking vessel made of griffin claws was reputed to change color if the liquid it contained was poisoned. The only way a griffin claw could be obtained, according to legend, was if a holy man received the claw in exchange for curing a griffin of some illness. Both a "griffin's claw" (actually the horn of an ibex) and a "griffin's egg" are on display in the British Museum.

It was also believed that a griffin feather, like the feathers of the phoenix, the firebird, and other fabulous birds, had magical powers. Many stories, like the two that follow, are built around the quest for griffin feathers.

The Old Griffin

German Folktale

In this wandering, lighthearted tale from the collection of the Brothers Grimm, folk traditions transform the griffin into an ogre with magic feathers. The wisdom of this Old Griffin is akin to that of the Persian Simurgh, the wise Bird of Ages.

here was once a King, but where he reigned and how he was called I know nothing about. He had no son, only a Daughter, who was always ill, and no doctor could cure her; then it was prophesied to the King, that his Daughter would eat herself well with an apple. So he made it known all over the kingdom, whoever brought his Daughter some apples with which she should eat herself well should marry her and be King.

Now, a Peasant, who had three sons, heard of it; and he said to the eldest, "Go to the garden, take a basketful of those beautiful apples with the red cheeks, and carry them to the court. Perhaps the King's Daughter will be able to eat herself well with them: and then you can marry her and be King."

The chap did as he was bid, and took to the road. When he had walked a little while he met quite a little Iron Man, who asked him what he had in his basket. So Hele, for that was his name, said, "Frogs' legs!" The little man then said, "Well, so it shall be, and remain," and then went on.

At last Hele came to the castle, and had it announced that he had got some apples which would cure the Princess if she ate them. At that the King was mightily pleased, and had Hele in court. Oh, dear! when he opened it, instead of apples, he had frogs' legs in the basket, and they were kicking about still. The King got into a great rage, and had him kicked out of the castle. When he got home he told his Father how he had fared.

Then the Father sent his next son, whose name was Saeme, but it went just the same with him as with Hele. The little Iron Man met him very soon, and asked him what he had in the basket, and Saeme said, "Sow-thistles;" and the little Man said, "Well, so it shall be, and remain."

When he arrived at the King's castle, and said he had apples with which the King's Daughter could eat herself well, they would not let him in, and told him there had already been one who had made fools of them. But Saeme insisted he had really such apples; they should only let him in. At last they believed him, and took him before the King; but when he opened the basket he had nothing but sow-thistles. That annoyed the King most dreadfully, so that he had Saeme whipped out of the castle. When he got home he told them what had happened to him.

Then came the youngest boy, whom they had always called stupid Jack, and asked the Father whether he, too, might go with apples. "Yes," said the Father, "you are just the right sort of fellow; if the clever ones can't succeed, what will you be able to do?"

The boy did not believe it. "Well, Father, I will go too."

"Get away, you stupid chap!" said the Father, "you must wait till you grow wiser," and then turned his back upon him; but the boy tugged at his smock-frock behind, and said, "Now Father, I will go too."

"Well, just as you like; go—you will be sure to come back," he answered in a spiteful way.

The boy was beyond measure delighted, and jumped for joy. "Ay, there! act like a fool! You get stupider from one day to the next," said the Father. That did not affect Jack a bit, who would not be disturbed in his joy.

As night soon came on, he thought he would wait the next morning; anyhow, he would not be able to get to court that day. He could not sleep that night in bed, and when he only slumbered a little he dreamed of beautiful maidens, of castles, gold, silver, and all that sort of thing.

Early next morning he went his way and soon the Little Man in his iron dress met him and asked him what he had in the basket. "Apples," he answered, "with which the King's Daughter should eat herself well." "Well," said the Little Man, "such it shall be, and remain."

But at court they would not let Jack in at all; for that there had been two who had said they brought apples, and one had frogs' legs, and the other sow-thistles. But Jack insisted tremendously he had no frogs' legs, but the most beautiful apples that grew in the kingdom. As he spoke so nicely the doorkeeper thought he could not be telling a lie, and let him in; and they did quite right too, for, when Jack uncovered the basket before the King, apples as yellow as gold came tumbling out.

The King was delighted, and had some of them taken to his Daughter at once, and waited in anxious expectation until they should bring him word what effect they had. Not long after news is brought him; but what think you it was? It was the Daughter herself! As soon as she had ate of those apples she had jumped out of bed quite well. What the King's delight was cannot be described.

But now the King would not give Jack his daughter to marry, and said that he must first make him a boat that would swim better on land than in the water. Jack agreed to the condition and went home and told his adventures.

So the Father sent Hele into the wood to make such a boat; he worked away diligently, and whistled the while. At midday, when the sun was at the highest, came the little Iron Man, and asked what he was making. "Wooden bowls," answered he. The little Man answered, "Well, so it shall be, and remain." In the evening Hele thought he had made the boat; but, when he was going to get into it, it turned to wooden bowls.

The next day Saeme went into the wood; but he met with exactly the same fate as his brother.

On the third day stupid Jack went: he worked very hard, so that the wood resounded all through with his heavy blows, and he sang and whistled besides right merrily. The little man came to him at midday when it was the hottest, and asked him what he was making. "A boat that will swim better on dry land than in the water," he answered, "and that when he had done it he should marry the King's Daughter." "Well," said the little Man, "such a one it shall be, and remain."

In the evening, when the sun was setting like a ball of gold, Jack made ready his boat and all things belonging to it, and rowed towards the castle; but the boat went as fast as the wind.

The King saw it a long way off; but would not give Jack his Daughter yet, and said he must first take a hundred hares out grazing from early morning to late in the evening, and if one were missing he should not have his Daughter. Jack was quite contented, and the next day went out with his herd to the meadow, and kept a sharp look-out that none should stray away.

Not many hours had passed when a Maid came from the castle, and said Jack was to give her a hare directly, as some visitors had arrived. But Jack saw through that well enough, and said he would not give her one; the King might treat his visitors to hare-pepper. But the Maid did not believe him and at last set to scolding. So Jack said that if the King's Daughter came herself he would give her a hare. The Maid told them in the castle, and the King's Daughter did go herself.

But in the meantime the little Man had come again to Jack and asked him what he was doing there. "Oh, he had got to watch a hundred hares so that none ran away, and then he might marry the King's Daughter, and be King." "Good!" said the little Man, "there's a whistle for you, and when one runs away only just whistle and he will come back again."

When the King's Daughter came, Jack gave her a hare into her apron. But when she had got about a hundred steps off, Jack whistled, and the hare jumped out of the cloth, and jump, jump! was back to the herd directly. In the evening the hare-herd whistled again, and looked to see they were all right, and drove them to the castle.

The King wondered how Jack had been able to take care of a hundred hares, so that none should run off: but he would not yet give him his Daughter so easily, but said he must first get him a feather from the Old Griffin's tail.

Jack started at once, and marched right briskly on. In the evening he arrived at a castle, where he asked for a night's lodging, for at that time there were no such things as hotels; and the master of the castle greeted him very civilly, and asked him where he was going to.

Jack answered, "To the Old Griffin."

"Oh, indeed! to the Old Griffin; they say he knows everything, and I have lost the key to an iron money-chest; perhaps you would be good enough to ask him where it is!"

"Certainly," said Jack, "that I will."

Early the next morning he started off again on his road, and arrived at another castle, where he again passed the night. When the people learned that he was going to the Old Griffin, they said a daughter was ill in the house; they had already tried every possible remedy, but without effect; would he be kind enough to ask Old Griffin what would cure her? Jack said he would do it with pleasure, and went on again.

He arrived at a lake; and, instead of a ferry-boat, there was a big man who had to carry everybody over. The Man asked him where he was bound for?

"To the Old Griffin," said Jack.

"When you get to him," said the Man, "just ask him why I am obliged to carry everybody over the water."

"Yes, to be sure," said Jack; "goodness gracious! yes, willingly!" The Man then took him up on his shoulder, and carried him over.

At last Jack arrived at the Old Griffin's house, and only found the wife at home—not the Old Griffin. The woman asked him what he wanted, so he told her he must have a feather from Old Griffin's tail; and that in the castle they had lost the key to the money-chest, and he was to ask the Griffin where it was; and then, in another castle the daughter was ill, and he was to know what would make her well again; then not far from there was the water, and the man who was obliged to carry everybody over, and he should very much like to know why the man was obliged to carry everybody over.

"But," said the Woman, "look you, my good friend, no Christian can speak with a Griffin; he eats them all up; but, if you like, you can reach out and pull a feather out of his tail; and as to those things that you want to know, I will ask him myself." Jack was quite satisfied with the arrangement, and got under the bed.

In the evening Old Griffin came home, and when he stepped into the room he said, "Wife, I smell a Christian!"

"Yes," said the Wife, "there has been one here to-day, but he went away again."

So Old Griffin said no more. In the middle of the night, when Griffin was snoring away lustily, Jack reached up and pulled a feather out of his tail.

The Griffin jumped up suddenly, and cried, "Wife, I smell a Christian! and it was just as if someone had been plucking at my tail."

The Wife said, "You have no doubt been dreaming. I have told you already that one has been here today, but that he went away again. He told me all sorts of things: that in one castle they had lost the key of the money-chest, and could not find it."

"Oh, the fools!" exclaimed the Griffin; "the key lies in the wood-shed, behind the door, under a log of wood."

"And, further, he said that in another castle the daughter was ill, and they knew no means to cure her."

"Oh, the fools!" said the Griffin, "under the cellar stairs a toad has made its nest of her hair, and if she got the hair back again she would be well."

"And then, again, he said, at a certain place there was a lake, and a man who was obliged to carry everybody over."

"Oh, the fool!" said the Old Griffin, "if he were only to put somebody into the middle he need not carry any more over."

Early next morning the Old Griffin got up and went out, and Jack crept from under the bed with a beautiful feather, having heard what the Griffin had said about the key, the daughter, and the man. The Wife repeated it all to him so he should not forget, and then he started off towards home.

He came to the man at the water first, and he asked him directly what the Griffin had said; but Jack said he must carry him over first, and then he would tell him. So he carried him over; and when they got there Jack told him he had only to put somebody into the middle and then he need carry no more. The man was delighted beyond measure, and told Jack that out of gratitude he should like to carry him over and back once more. But Jack said nay, he would save him the trouble; he was quite contented with him already, and then went on.

Then he arrived at the castle where the daughter was ill; he took her on his shoulder, for she was not able to walk, and carried her down the cellar stairs, and then took the toad's nest from under the bottom step, and put it into the daughter's hand, and all at once she jumped off his shoulder, up the stairs before him, strong and well. Now the father and mother were delighted indeed, and made Jack presents of gold and silver, and whatever he wanted, they gave him.

When Jack arrived at the other castle he went straight to the wood-shed, and found the key right enough behind the door, under the log of wood, and took it to the master. He was not a little pleased, and gave Jack in return a great deal of gold that was in the box, and all sorts of things besides, such as cows, and sheep, and goats.

When Jack returned to the King with all these things, with the money, and gold, and silver, and the cows, sheep, and goats, the King asked him where ever he had come by it all. So Jack said the Old Griffin would give one as much as one liked. The King thought he could find a use for that sort of thing himself, and so started off to the Griffin; but when he got to the water he happened to be the first who arrived there since Jack, and the man put him in the middle and walked off, and the King was drowned.

So Jack married the King's Daughter and became King.

From *The Complete Illustrated Stories of the Brothers Grimm*. London, 1853; Reprint, Octopus Books, 1984.

The Griffon

Italian Fairy Tale

Both the quest for a magic feather and the "singing bone" that tells the truth are found in many fairy tales. Here, in a story retold by Peter Lum (Bettina Lum Crowe) in her Italian Fairy Tales, *the two themes are combined.*

ntil quite recently Italy, as we know, was divided into a number of separate kingdoms or princedoms, each with its own ruler. Now the King of one such kingdom, in northern Italy, was blind. He had lost his sight gradually, and he had never given up hope that his blindness was temporary and that he might one day be able to see again.

As the years went by he tried every possible treatment for his blindness, without success. Then at last a doctor in whom he had great confidence told him that there was one thing, and one thing only, which would ever restore his sight. If he could manage to obtain a feather from the wings of a griffon, dip it in oil, and anoint his eyelids he would be cured.

This was by no means as easy as it sounds. The Griffon is a fabulous creature, half bird and half animal, who lives far away in the eastern mountains, in the direction of Persia, where the sun rises. He is sometimes called the Bird of the Sun, or Bird of Light, instead of the Griffon, and it is because he lives so close to the sun that his feathers have the magic property of restoring sight to the blind.

Many men, during many hundreds of years, have come from different parts of the world in search of this remarkable bird. They have sought him for two reasons. First, because the touch of any one of his feathers can cure blindness. And secondly, because the claw of a griffon, like the horn of a Unicorn, will immediately detect the presence of poison in any liquid, whatever it may be. A man who was lucky enough to find or steal a Griffon's claw would have it made into a drinking cup, and drink only from that cup; he knew that if an enemy ever put poison in his drink, the cup would at once darken, change colour, and become covered in sweat.

The Griffon, however, is an elusive bird, and fierce, and will not easily part with either a feather or a claw. Few of the men who hunted him had even caught a glimpse of him. Far fewer came within reach of him, or succeeded in carrying off a feather from his wing.

The blind King had three sons, who were not grown up. When he was told that nothing could possibly restore his sight except the feather of a Griffon he called his sons together and asked them all three to set forth in search of such a feather. At the same time he promised them that whoever first secured the Griffon's feather and brought it back to him should inherit the whole of his kingdom.

The three sons set off towards the sunrise. The two older Princes travelled together, being inclined to linger and enjoy themselves along the way. After all, they thought to themselves, it was most unlikely that they could ever find the magic bird, let alone pluck a feather from its wing. They had no liking for adventure, certainly not for such a hopeless quest as this. They would go as far as the first foothills of the Persian mountains, they decided, and then turn back and tell their father that it was impossible; sooner or later he would die and they would inherit the kingdom in any case. But the younger son walked and walked and walked towards the sunrise, as straight and as fast as his feet would carry him.

It was not long before the young Prince saw the eastern mountains rising high in front of him. They were still a long way off and they were the most forbidding mountains he had ever seen, steep, rocky and barren of all vegetation. His heart sank when he saw them, and his courage almost failed him when he thought of trying to penetrate into that wilderness. Nevertheless he walked on, and on, day after day.

As he drew near to the edge of the mountains he met an old man. They greeted each other warmly, as travellers do in such lonesome parts of the world, and talked together for a little while about the weather, and the time of year, and how cold it must be in the high mountains.

"Where are you going?" the old man asked him curiously. "Not many people travel this way."

"I am going to the mountains where the sun rises, to find the Griffon and pluck a feather from his wing, so that my father the King may regain his sight," said the young Prince, and he sighed. "I am afraid it will not be easy. They say that the Griffon is a wild, fierce bird."

"It is true that he does not like to be disturbed," said the old man. "But he is also greedy. I can tell you how to steal a feather from his wing."

"Tell me," said the Prince.

"You must take this handful of corn"—and the man gave him a small measure of grain—"And when you come to a certain place in the mountains, not far from here, which I will show you, you must sit down on the ground and put the corn in your hat. If you sit there long enough and still enough, like a statue, the Griffon will not realize that you are alive and he will eventually come flying down to eat the corn. Then you must seize him very quickly by the leg. You will not be able to hold him long, for he has strong wings and powerful claws, but you should have enough time to pull one feather out of his wing. As soon as you have done so throw yourself flat on your face on the ground and do not move a muscle until the Griffon is out of sight; otherwise he might well lift you up and carry you off with him into the mountains. I have seen him carry away an ox before now."

These last words did not altogether reassure the young Prince. Nevertheless he thanked the man warmly, took the corn, and went on his way to the place in the mountains which his benefactor had pointed out to him. There he sat down on the ground, put the corn in his hat, and waited. He sat motionless, like a statue, scarcely daring to breathe, and waited.

It all came to pass as the old man had foretold. Suddenly there was a great rush of wings, the sky overhead was darkened, and he could feel that a huge bird was hovering above him, pecking at the grains of corn in his hat. He dared not look up. Instead he slowly, slowly raised one hand and grabbed the bird by its leg. Then he quickly put out his other hand and clutched a feather from its wing. The bird gave a great shriek, struck at the young Prince's hat with his claws, and soared away up into the air. The Prince was left holding the feather.

He threw himself flat on the ground and lay there for what seemed a very long time. Then he rolled over on his back and looked around him. The sky was clear, without a cloud, the mountains were as barren and empty as ever; there was no sign of a bird, nor anything to show that one had ever been there. Nothing, that is, except the one precious feather he was holding in his hand.

Overjoyed by his success, the young Prince hid the feather in his left shoe to make sure that it was neither lost nor stolen, and set off for home. He had only gone a short distance when he met his two older brothers, who had just come within sight of the eastern mountains and were not thinking that it was time to turn back. The two brothers recognized him from far away, and the one said to the other: "See how proudly our young brother walks, as though he had the whole world beneath his feet. He must have found the feather."

"You are right," said the second son; "He has certainly found it."

The Griffin

They walked a few paces in silence. Then the first son said to the other: "Let us take the feather from him, and kill him, and leave his body here. We will tell our father the King that we two have secured the feather for him, and he will divide the kingdom between us."

"You are right," said his brother. "That is what we will do."

When the brothers had come up to each other, and greeted one another, the eldest asked the youngest whether he had found the Griffon's feather. Suspecting treachery, he said no, he had not found it. But the other two would not believe him. They fell on him and stripped him and searched his clothing, and at last they found the feather hidden in his left shoe. Then they killed him, buried his body there on the edge of the eastern mountains, and hurried home in triumph to give their father the feather and to claim the kingdom.

The old King dipped the Griffon's feather in oil and brushed it across his eyelids. Immediately he opened his eyes and he could see. He was so delighted that he embraced his two older sons, praised them for their courage, and divided the kingdom between them there and then. Somewhat later, he asked them about their younger brother.

"I thought you travelled to the mountains together?" he said. "Why do you suppose he has not yet returned?"

"We travelled a little way together," said the eldest Prince, "but our young brother seemed to be in no hurry; he was enjoying himself along the way. So we finally left him behind, hurrying on toward the mountains of sunrise by ourselves."

"And you did not meet him anywhere on your way home?"

"No," the second Prince assured his father. "We were anxious to bring you the feather as quickly as possible so we took the shortest road. Our young brother probably turned aside somewhere to rest, or to amuse himself."

As days and weeks and months went by and the young Prince did not return, the King reluctantly came to the conclusion that he must have been waylaid, or met with some accident. Perhaps if he had ever reached the land of the sun the Griffon had killed him, or carried him away to its lair in the farther mountains. The old King mourned his loss. But he was so delighted to have regained his sight that he could not be unhappy for long, and he thought less and less about the missing Prince.

Meanwhile in the eastern mountains a young shepherd who was in the habit of pasturing his sheep in the foothills thereabouts noticed that his sheepdog was always sniffing around and digging at one particular place. Wondering what the dog had found, and whether some treasure might not be buried there, the shepherd began to dig at that spot. He dug, and dug, until he had dug a deep hole, but all that he found was one small bone. It was a curious bone, shaped so exactly like a whistle that the shepherd, almost without thinking, put it to his lips. Immediately he heard a low whisper from the bone:

"Shepherd, keep me in your mouth, hold me tight, and do not let me go. For a feather of the Griffon, my brothers have played the traitor, have played the traitor"—and the whisper died away in a plaintive echo—"The traitor, the traitor, the traitor...."

Astonished by this voice, although he had no idea what it meant, the shepherd kept the whistle and carried it with him wherever he went. Whenever he placed it in his mouth he heard the words repeated over and over again.

This same shepherd was in the habit of trading his sheep far and wide, in every part of the country. So it happened that in time he came to the city of the once-blind King, and passed by the royal palace on his way to the market. He had the whistle in his mouth at the time. The King, looking out of his window, saw the flock of sheep go by and heard a strange whistle, apparently coming from the lips of the shepherd, as they passed; it was a sound unlike any he had ever heard, more like the moaning of the wind than a shepherd's tune. Curious, he ordered his servants to bring the man up to the gate of the palace, where he could speak to him.

"What are these words you keep whispering to yourself as you drive your sheep to market?" he asked.

"I do not whisper them, Your Majesty," the shepherd assured him. "It is this bone, like a whistle, that I found in the mountains." And he told him the story of his sheepdog, and how he himself had dug into the earth in search of treasure and unearthed the bone instead.

The King took the bone, looked at it with interest, and placed it in his own mouth. "Papa!" he heard, "Papa! Keep me in your mouth, hold me tight, and do not let me go. For a feather of the Griffon, my brothers have played the traitor, have played the traitor, the traitor...."

"What on earth does this mean?" cried the King, horrified. "Is it possible that my older sons betrayed their brother for the sake of the feather they brought me, and the kingdom I promised them?"

He questioned the shepherd more closely about when and where he had found the bone. "In the foothills of the eastern mountains, the mountains of the sun," the man replied. "Not far from the land of the Griffon."

The King now called his oldest son, who had already succeeded to half of the kingdom. Without a word of explanation he asked him to put the whistle to his lips for a moment. No sooner had it touched his lips than the Prince, the King and the shepherd could all hear the voice, which seemed louder now, crying out: "Brother! Brother! Keep me in your mouth, hold me tight, and do not let me go. For a feather of the Griffon, you have played the traitor, have played the traitor...."

"What is this nonsense?" cried the Prince. But he had turned white as a ghost, and he pulled the whistle out of his mouth and threw it violently away into some bushes nearby. The shepherd quickly went and picked it up again, handing it back to the King.

Thereupon the King called his second son, who had succeeded to the other half of the kingdom. He commanded him to put the whistle to his lips. Exactly the same thing happened all over again. The two Princes stared at each other in horror as they realized that somehow the truth was known. And the King took the whistle in his hands again, and wept, for now he knew what fate had befallen his youngest son. Indeed the two conspirators soon confessed the whole story; they could scarcely deny their guilt when the evidence had come from their own lips.

The King condemned his two sons to death, and they were executed. But, alas, he had no means of restoring the younger boy to life. All he could do was to carry the whistle with him as long as he lived, listening to its plaintive echo and lamenting the death of the brave Prince who had actually succeeded in obtaining the Griffon's feather for him and thus restoring his sight. He no longer took any great pleasure in the fact that he could see. He would gladly have been blind again, he sometimes thought to himself, if he could have had his youngest son beside him once again.

That is the end of the story, according to some storytellers. Others say that although he could not bring his own son back to life, the old King did not die without an heir to the throne. He adopted the shepherd who had brought him the whistling bone as his son and heir. And this youth, so they say, came to resemble the dead Prince more and more as the years went by; he finally inherited the whole of the kingdom and ruled wisely and well for a long, long time.

From *Italian Fairy Tales* by Peter Lum. Chicago: Follett, 1963, pp. 150-160. Copyright © 1963 by Peter Lum.

The Griffin Today

The fabulous beast that pulled the chariots of deities and kings and guarded gold and royal tombs is an enduring majestic image.

A major figure in heraldry since the Middle Ages, the griffin is still very much with us today, though it is not always easy to recognize. It is just one more of a host of ornamental monsters until one becomes acquainted with its eagle-lion shape. Then it seems to be everywhere: on Peerless Tyres signs, publishers' logos, business cards, key chains, antique fireplaces and furniture, cathedrals, balcony railings, covers of art books and fantasy paperbacks. It is on knights' shields in adventure films and is in artifacts of bronze and gold and precious stones in museum cases throughout the Western world. Tourists daily peer into a chamber of the Palace of Minos at Knossos, Crete, and see the graceful painted griffins guarding the throne of the king.

Two hundred years after Sir Thomas Browne denied its existence, the griffin reappeared in children's literature, notably as Lewis Carroll's raving, comic animal. The beast has been a familiar figure ever since in both children's stories and fantasy novels, unique in its strength and its nobility.

Alice, the Gryphon, and the Mock Turtle

Lewis Carroll

In Alice's Adventures in Wonderland, *Lewis Carroll (1822-1898) transformed the grand griffin of old into a comic figure dancing on the seashore with the Mock Turtle. John Tenniel's illustration of the sleeping griffin may well be the definitive rendering of the magnificent beast.*

hey very soon came upon a Gryphon, lying fast asleep in the sun. (If you don't know what a Gryphon is, look at the picture.) "Up, lazy thing!" said the Queen, "and take this young lady to see the Mock Turtle, and to hear his history. I must go back and see after some executions I have ordered;" and she walked off, leaving Alice alone with the Gryphon. Alice did not quite like the look of the creature, but on the whole she thought it would be quite as safe to stay with it as to go after that savage Queen: so she waited.

The Gryphon sat up and rubbed its eyes; then it watched the Queen till she was out of sight: then it chuckled. "What fun!" said the Gryphon, half to itself, half to Alice.

"What *is* the fun?" said Alice.

"Why, *she*," said the Gryphon. "It's all her fancy, that: they never executes nobody, you know. Come on!"

"Everybody says 'come on!' here," thought Alice, as she went slowly after it: "I never was so ordered about before, in all my life, never!"

They had not gone far before they saw the Mock Turtle in the distance, sitting sad and lonely on a little ledge of rock, and, as they came nearer, Alice could hear him sighing as if his heart would break. She pitied him deeply. "What is his sorrow?" she asked the Gryphon. And the Gryphon answered, very nearly in the same words as before, "It's all his fancy, that: he hasn't got no sorrow, you know. Come on!"

So they went up to the Mock Turtle, who looked at them with large eyes full of tears, but said nothing.

* * *

The Mock Turtle sighed deeply, and drew the back of one flapper across his eyes. He looked at Alice and tried to speak, but, for a minute or two, sobs choked his voice. "Same as if he had a bone in his throat," said the Gryphon; and it set to work shaking him and punching him in the back. At last the Mock Turtle recovered his voice, and, with tears running down his cheeks, he went on again:

"You may not have lived much under the sea—" ("I haven't," said Alice)—"and perhaps you were never even introduced to a lobster—" (Alice began to say "I once tasted—" but checked herself hastily, and said "No, never") "—so you can have no idea what a delightful thing a Lobster-Quadrille is!"

"No, indeed," said Alice. "What sort of a dance is it?"

"Why," said the Gryphon, "you first form into a line along the sea-shore—"

"Two lines!" cried the Mock Turtle. "Seals, turtles, salmon, and so on: then, when you've cleared all the jellyfish out of the way—"

"*That* generally takes some time," interrupted the Gryphon.

"—you advance twice——"

"Each with a lobster as a partner!" cried the Gryphon.

John Tenniel's sleeping griffin from *Alice's Adventures in Wonderland.*

"Of course," the Mock Turtle said: "advance twice, set to partners——"

"—change lobsters, and retire in same order," continued the Gryphon.

"Then, you know," the Mock Turtle went on, "you throw the——"

"The lobsters!" shouted the Gryphon, with a bound into the air.

"—as far out to sea as you can——"

"Swim after them!" screamed the Gryphon.

"Turn a somersault in the sea!" cried the Mock Turtle, capering wildly about.

"Change lobsters again!" yelled the Gryphon at the top of its voice.

"Back to land again, and—that's all the first figure," said the Mock Turtle, suddenly dropping his voice; and the two creatures, who had been jumping about like mad things all this time, sat down again very sadly and quietly, and looked at Alice.

From *Alice's Adventures in Wonderland* by Lewis Carroll. Chicago: M. A. Donahue, 1904.

The Unicorn

The Unicorn

he mysterious equine creature with cloven hooves and a single spiral horn glides silently through our imagination. Pure and eternal, the unicorn roams free in misty woods of legend, its magical horn graced with curative powers.

Some said it was a ferocious beast of the mountains that could never be taken alive. In older paintings, it is often one of the animals grazing in the Garden of Eden, and in medieval legend it is charmed only by fair young virgins. It glows milky white in lush medieval tapestries, sometimes honoring noble ladies, sometimes being captured and even killed by hunters.

Many claimed to have seen the animal, from the Temple at Mecca to the wilds of Africa. What was said to be its prized horn sold for small fortunes in apothecary shops and was displayed in cathedrals and in glass museum cases.

As the constellation Monoceros, the unicorn moves silently and faintly within the misty band of the Milky Way. The magical animal can also be found in pewter and glass in gift shop windows. It wanders through heraldry, children's literature, modern fantasy, and reverie.

The Unicorn from the Past

When compared with a mountain sheep, a longhorn cow, a reindeer, a bull moose, and other horned animals, the figure we think of as a unicorn hardly seems fantastic. It has a single straight horn growing out of its forehead, no curling headpiece, or horns with graceful curves, no tree-like branches or rack spread out like an open human hand. Nor does the unicorn seem so unusual when compared with other animals with single horns, creatures as diverse as the rhinoceros, the narwhal, and the unicorn beetle.

Legends of the unicorn may, in fact, have had their origin in the rhinoceros, but time transformed the animal from a wild, ferocious beast into an elegant, mysterious, and magical creature.

Ancient Unicorns

The earliest description we have of the unicorn is by Ctesias, a Greek physician at the Persian court. In his book on the wonders of India, the unicorn had a white body, a dark red head, and blue eyes. Its horn, the length of a forearm, was white, black in the middle, and bright red on the tip. Four hundred years later, Pliny's unicorn was a horse-like creature with the head of a deer, the feet of an elephant, the tail of a swine, and a black horn three feet long.

One reason people believed in the unicorn for so long was that the Greek philosopher Aristotle stated that there were two kinds of one-horned animals: the oryx and an Indian beast which was probably the rhinoceros. Another authoritative reference was by Julius Caesar. In his chronicle of the Gallic Wars, he wrote that in the Hercynian Forest near the Rhine lived a stag-like creature that had a single long horn growing out of its forehead.

Some reports of one-horned animals are thought to be from people who observed them in profile or saw an animal whose other horn had broken off. Many of the early accounts of the unicorn may be based on misleading descriptions of the rhinoceros, sometimes called the *Cartazonus*.

Medieval Unicorns

A different kind of animal that came to be identified with a unicorn was the wild ox. The fierce *reem* of the Bible became *monoceros* and *unicornus* in some translations, leading to "unicorn" in a modern version. Emphasizing its strength and purity, Church fathers and bestiary writers made the unicorn a spiritual symbol.

In secular romances and legend, the unicorn figured in tales of three famous warriors: King Arthur, Genghis Khan, and Alexander the Great.

King Arthur's ship, the story goes, was once blown onto a strange coast where a dwarf told him that his son and he were being cared for by a mother unicorn in the forest. Having been raised on unicorn milk, the son grew into a giant and built the square red tower in which he and his father lived. After Arthur was honored with a feast in the tower, the giant and the unicorn

Bestiary unicorn. (Illustration by Joan Garner.)

---

dragged the King's grounded ship off the shore, and they all sailed off to England.

The conqueror Genghis Khan was ready to invade India when a unicorn appeared before one of his commanders and told him that his leader should return to his own land. Years of bloodshed behind him, Genghis Khan relented, allowing India to be saved by a unicorn.

According to one story, Bucephalus, the horse of Alexander the Great, was a unicorn with the tail of a peacock. Bucephalus withdrew from a battle near the Red Sea, when unicorns attacked the troops of Alexander and were destroyed.

Two famous series of symbolic tapestries—both thought to have been created in Brussels circa 1500—depict the unicorn much as we have come to think of it today. By then the creature had become a graceful white horse-like creature with cloven hooves, the beard of a goat, and a long spiraling white horn. The tapestries can still be seen in museums in New York and Paris.

In *The Hunt of the Unicorn*, hunters come upon the unicorn at a fountain as it purifies the water with its horn. After it fends off the hunters with horn and hooves, it is deceived by a beautiful maiden. The hunters brutally kill the beast, but in the final tapestry, the unicorn is alive again, sitting proudly inside a fence within a flowering garden.

In *The Lady and the Unicorn*, the unicorn and its traditional enemy, the lion, pose heraldically on either side of a noblewoman. Each of the first five panels of the six-panel series represents one of the senses: hearing, sight, smell, taste, and touch.

Behind the pairing of the lion and the unicorn is the history of their combat. In the traditional story, as related in the Letter of Prester John, the lion provokes the unicorn into chasing it. As the two run at full

Unicorn from *The Lady and the Unicorn* tapestry.

speed, the unicorn in hot pursuit, the lion heads toward a tree. At the last second, the lion swerves; the unicorn's horn drives deeply into the wood, and the lion slays its trapped enemy. Later, in the Grimm Brothers' "Brave Little Tailor," the tailor captures a unicorn in a similar manner by leaping behind a tree when the creature charges him.

Heraldic unicorn.

The lion and the unicorn appear together in heraldry as supporters of England and Scotland in the royal arms of both countries. The lion represents England and the unicorn Scotland. The heraldic unicorn has the head, mane, and body of a horse; the legs and hooves of a deer; the tail of a lion; a beard; and a long, twisted horn. Until the seventeenth century, the unicorn was considered an actual animal in heraldry, not a mythical beast.

What may be the most famous eyewitness description of unicorns was published only a few years after the unicorn tapestries were made. In his book of travels in the Near East, the Italian Lewis Vartoman told of one-horned animals in the holy temple of Mecca and in the city of Zeila.

Alicorn

From ancient times up to a few hundred years ago, unicorn horn, or alicorn, was widely believed to prevent or cure sickness. Ctesias wrote that people who drank from cups of unicorn horn were safe from poison and certain diseases. Over time, unicorn horn became regarded as a cure-all, and it literally came to be worth its weight in gold. Powdered alicorn was sold in apothecary shops, and the rich purchased entire horns for small fortunes. To test whether a horn was genuine, the horn was used to draw a circle on the ground, and a spider was set inside; if the spider did not crawl out of the circle, the horn was considered real. Alicorn often turned out to be the single tusk of the narwhal (*Monodon monoceros*).

Heraldic unicorn.

Believers and Skeptics

Except for a few dissenting voices, the unicorn was alive and well up into the seventeenth century. The monumental natural histories of Konrad Gesner, Ulysses Aldrovandi, and Edward Topsell contained extended chapters on the animal, repeating the stories of the ancient and medieval writers. Also, many travelers through the centuries either claimed to have seen one-horned animals (other than the rhinoceros) or were told about them by others who said they had seen such creatures.

Heraldic unicorn.

As was true of other animals we now consider fabulous, though, not everyone was convinced that there was an actual white creature with a single magical horn projecting from its forehead. One of those skeptical about the existence of the unicorn and the power of its horn was a famous sixteenth-century French physician, Ambroise Paré. In his book, *Of Poisons*, he wrote:

> I think that beast that is vulgarly called and taken for a Unicorn is rather a thing imaginary than really in the world. I am chiefly induced to believe thus by these conjectures. Because of those who have travelled over the world, there is not one that professeth that ever he did see that creature. . . . For these that have written of the Unicorn, either that they have heard, or that hath been delivered by tradition, or what they in their own minds and fancies have conceived, you shall scarce find two that agree together, either in the description of the body, or in the nature and condition of her.

Heraldic unicorn.

Later, in Shakespeare's *Tempest*, it is clear that the sophisticated members of the royal shipwrecked party do not accept the existence of either the phoenix or the unicorn. Sebastian, the brother of the King of Naples, is so astonished at the magic of Prospero's island that he says:

Now I will believe
That there are unicorns; that in Arabia
There is one tree, the phoenix' throne; one phoenix
At this hour reigning there.

The unicorn came under more and more scholarly attacks until it was dismissed—for a time—as a mere fanciful creature. But the Western world had not seen the last of this magical animal.

The Wild Unicorns of India

Ctesias

The first known description of the unicorn, and of its magical horn, is from Indica, *a book on the marvels of India, by Ctesias [Kuh-TEE-see-us], early fifth century B.C. Pliny used this passage in his account of the wonder beasts of Ethiopia. To the ancients, "India" was a name for the vast lands to the east, and "Ethiopia" for the land mass to the south of Egypt. The names of the two areas were often confused with each other and used interchangeably. The "sacred disease" is epilepsy, and the "huckle-bone" is a hipbone.*

 mong the Indians, . . . there are wild asses as large as horses, some being even larger. Their head is of a dark red colour, their eyes blue, and the rest of their body white. They have a horn on their forehead, a cubit in length. This horn for about two palm-breadths upwards from the base is of the purest white, where it tapers to a sharp point of a flaming crimson, and, in the middle, is black. These horns are made into drinking cups, and such as drink from them are attacked neither by convulsions nor by the sacred disease. Nay, they are not even affected by poisons, if either before or after swallowing them they drink from these cups wine, water, or anything else. While other asses moreover, whether wild or tame, and indeed all other solid-hoofed animals have neither huckle-bones, nor gall in the liver, these one-horned asses have both. Their huckle-bone is the most beautiful of all I have ever seen, and is, in appearance and size, like that of the ox. It is as heavy as lead, and of the colour of cinnabar both on the surface, and all throughout. It is exceedingly fleet and strong, and no creature that pursues it, not even the horse, can overtake it.

On first starting it scampers off somewhat leisurely, but the longer it runs, it gallops faster and faster till the pace becomes most furious. These animals therefore can only be caught at one particular time—that is when they lead out their little foals to the pastures in which they roam. They are then hemmed in on all sides by a vast number of hunters mounted on horseback, and being unwilling to escape while leaving their young to perish, stand their ground and fight, and by butting with their horns and kicking and biting kill many horses and men. But they are in the end taken, pierced to death with arrows and spears, for to take them alive is in no way possible. Their flesh being bitter is unfit for food, and they are hunted merely for the sake of their horns and their huckle-bones.

From *Ancient India: As Described by Ktêsias the Knidian*, translated by J. W. McCrindle. Delhi, India: Manohar Reprints, 1973, pp. 26-27.

The Unicorns of Basma

Marco Polo

Because of its horn, the rhinoceros and the legendary unicorn were often confused with one another. Describing the unicorn in his celebrated Travels, *Marco Polo carefully distinguishes the Asian rhinoceros from the beast of fable. Even so, his description of the rhinoceros is a composite of several animals, in the standard manner of early travel writers. Ferlec and Basma were areas in what is now the Indonesian island of Sumatra.*

hen you quit the kingdom of Ferlec you enter upon that of Basma. . . . There are wild elephants in the country, and numerous unicorns, which are very nearly as big. They have hair like that of a buffalo, feet like those of an elephant, and a horn in the middle of the forehead, which is black and very thick. They do no mischief, however, with the horn, but with the tongue alone; for this is covered all over with long and strong prickles (and when savage with any one they crush him under their knees and then rasp him with their tongue). The head resembles that of a wild boar, and they carry it ever bent towards the ground. They delight much to abide in mire and mud. 'Tis a passing ugly beast to look upon, and is not in the least like that which our stories tell of as being caught in the lap of a virgin; in fact, 'tis altogether different from what we fancied.

From *The Travels of Marco Polo*, translated by Sir Henry Yule and edited by Henri Cordier. London: John Murray, 1903. Reprint, New York: Dover Books, 1993, p. 285.

Unicorns in Mecca and Zeila

Lewis Vartoman

The most famous eyewitness descriptions of unicorns were by the early sixteenth-century Italian traveler, Lewis Vartoman (Ludovico di Varthema). Vartoman is said to be the first European to enter the holy city of Mecca. In his Travels, *Vartoman describes the "unicorns" he saw in the Temple of Mecca and in the city of Zeila, which was in what was called Ethiopia and is now in modern Somalia. "Braccio," "palmo," and "brazzo" are old Italian measurements, referring to arm's-length (about two feet), hand's-length (about six inches), and the reach of outspread arms (about five-and-a-half feet). Zerzalino is sesame, whose seeds yield oil.*

n another part of the said temple is an enclosed place in which there are two live unicorns, and these are shown as very remarkable objects, which they certainly are. I will tell you how they are made. The elder is formed like a colt of thirty months old, and he has a horn in the forehead, which horn is about three *braccia* in length. The other unicorn is like a colt of one year old, and he has a horn of about four *palmi* long. The colour of the said animal resembles that of a dark bay horse, and his head resembles that of a stag; his neck is not very long, and he has some thin and short hair which hangs on one side; his legs are slender and lean like those of a goat; the foot is a little cloven in the fore part, and long and goat-like, and there are some hairs on the hind part of the said legs. Truly this monster must be a very fierce and solitary animal. These two animals were presented to the Sultan of Mecca as the finest things that could be found in the world at the present day, and as the richest treasure ever sent by a king of Ethiopia, that is, by a Moorish king. He made this present in order to secure an alliance with the said Sultan of Mecca.

* * *

The . . . city of Zeila is a place of immense traffic, especially in gold and elephants' teeth. Here also are sold a very great number of slaves, which are those people of Prester John whom the Moors take in battle, and from this place they are carried into Persia, Arabia Felix, and to Mecca, Cairo, and into India. In this city people live extremely well, and justice is excellently administered. Much grain grows here and much animal food, oil in great quantity, made not from olives but from *zerzalino*, honey and wax in great abundance. Here is found a kind of sheep, the tails of which weigh fifteen or sixteen pounds, and with the head and neck quite black, but the whole of the rest of the body white. There are also some other sheep, which have tails a *brazzo* long and twisted like vines, and they have the dewlap like that of a bull, which almost touches the ground. Also in this place I found a certain kind of cows, which had horns like a stag and were wild, which had been presented to the Sultan of the said city. I also saw there other cows, which had a single horn in the forehead, which horn is a *palmo* and a half in length, and turns more towards the back of the cow than forwards. The colour of these is red, that of the former is black.

From *The Travels of Ludovico di Varthema*, translated by John Winter Jones. London: The Hakluyt Society, 1863, pp.46-49, 86-87.

The Unicorn

Edward Topsell

The English clergyman Edward Topsell (1572- 1625) freely mixed fabulous animals with actual ones in his Historie of Foure-Footed Beasts. *In his long chapter on the unicorn, Topsell sums up the major writings of the past to try to prove to his readers that such a marvelous animal really does exist. Among the authorities Topsell mentions are some who appear elsewhere in this book: Lewis Vartoman ("Ludovicus Romanus"), Julius Caesar, and Aelian. "Albertus" is Albertus Magnus, saint, philosopher, and author of a major natural history. "Articles" are joints. A "cratch" is a manger. "Decoction" is a boiled-down mixture. The following excerpts include Topsell's personal account of using unicorn horn as a medicine.*

e are now come to the history of a beast, whereof divers people in every age of the world have made great question, because of the rare virtues thereof; therefore it behoveth us to use some diligence in comparing together the several testimonies that are spoken of this beast, for the better satisfaction of such as are now alive, and clearing of the point for them that shall be

Unicorn (Edward Topsell).

born hereafter, whether there be a Unicorn; for that is the main question to be resolved.

Now the virtues of the horn, of which we will make a particular discourse by itself, have been the occasion of this question, and that which doth give the most evident testimony unto all men that have ever seen it or used it, hath bred all the contention; and if there had not been disclosed in it any extraordinary powers and virtues, we should as easily believe that there was a Unicorn in the world, as we do believe there is an Elephant although not bred in Europe. To begin therefore with this discourse, by the Unicorn we do understand a peculiar beast, which hath naturally but one horn, and that a very rich one, that groweth out of the middle of the forehead, for we have shewed in other parts of the history, that there are divers beasts, that have but one horn, and namely some Oxen in India have but one horn, and some have three, and whole hoofs. Likewise the Bulls of Aonia, are said to have whole hoofs and one horn, growing out of the middle of their foreheads.

Likewise in the City Zeila of Ethiopia, there are Kine of a purple colour, as Ludovicus Romanus writeth, which have but one horn growing out of their heads, and that turneth up towards their backs. Caesar was of opinion that the Elk had but one horn, but we have shewed the contrary. It is said that Pericles had a Ram with one horn, but that was bred by way of prodigy, and not naturally. Simeon Sethi writeth, that the Musk-cat hath also one horn growing out of the forehead, but we have shewed already that no man is of that opinion but himself. Aelianus writeth, that there be Birds in Aethiopia having one horn on their foreheads, and therefore are called Unicorns: and Albertus saith, there is a fish called Monoceros, and hath also one horn. Now our discourse of the Unicorn is of none of these beasts, for there is not any virtue attributed to their horns, and therefore the vulgar sort of Infidel people which scarcely believe any herb but such as they see in their own Gardens, or any beast but such as is in their own flocks, or any knowledge but such as is bred in their own brains, or any birds which are not hatched in their own nests, have never made question of these, but of the true Unicorn, whereof there were more proofs in the world, because of the nobleness of his horn, they have ever been in doubt.

* * *

These beasts are very swift, and their legs have no Articles. They keep for the most part in the Deserts, and live solitary in the tops of the Mountains. There was nothing more horrible then the voice or braying of it, for the voice is strained above measure. It fighteth both with the mouth and with the heels, with the mouth biting like a Lion, and with the heel kicking like a Horse. It is a beast of an untamable nature, and therefore the Lord himself in Job saith, that he cannot be tied with any halter, nor yet accustomed to any cratch or stable.

* * *

It is said by Aelianus and Albertus, that except they be taken before they be two years old they will never be tamed; and that the Thracians do yearly take some of their Colts, and bring them to the King, which he keepeth for combat, and to fight with one another: for when they are old, they differ nothing at all from the most barbarous, bloody, and ravenous beasts. Their flesh is not good for meat, but is bitter and unnourishable: And thus much shall suffice for the natural story of the Unicorn; now followeth the medicinal.

* * *

The horns of Unicorns, especially that which is brought from new Islands, being beaten and drunk in water, doth wonderfully help against poison: as of late experience doth manifest unto us, a man, who having taken poison and beginning to swell was preserved by this remedy. I myself have heard of a man worthy to be believed, that having eaten a poisoned cherry, and perceiving his belly to swell, he cured himself by the marrow of this horn being drunk in Wine, in very short space.

The same is also praised at this day for the curing of the Falling sickness, and affirmed by Aelianus, who called this disease cursed. The ancient Writers did attribute the force of healing to cups made of this horn, Wine being drunk out of them: but because we cannot have cups, we drink the substance of this horn, either by itself or with other medicines. I happily sometime made this Sugar of the horn, as they call it, mingling with the same Amber, Ivory dust, leaves of gold, coral, & certain other things, the horn being included in silk, and beaten in the decoction of Raisins and Cinnamon, I cast them in water, the rest of the reason of healing in the meantime not being neglected. . . . The horn of a Unicorn being beaten and boiled in Wine hath a wonderful effect in making the teeth white or clear, the mouth being well cleansed therewith. And thus much shall suffice for the medicines and virtues arising from the Unicorn.

From *The Historie of Foure-Footed Beasts* by Edward Topsell. London, 1658, pp. 551-52, 557-59.

The Unicorn Around the World

Besides the one-horned animals sighted by travelers and debated by scholars, fabulous relatives of the Western unicorn—both close and distant—roam through the legends and art of peoples around the globe. The white, mystical creature of later Western tradition appears in European folktales, while the unicorns of the Middle East and Asia have their own unique shapes and attributes.

The Ki-Lin

Along with the phoenix, the dragon, and the tortoise, the unicorn (the Ki-Lin, Ki-lin, k'i-lin) is one of the four great mythical animals of China, creatures of good omen.

The Ki-Lin has the body of a deer, hoofs of a horse, and tail of an ox. Unlike the milk-white unicorn of the West, its bright fur is red, yellow, blue, white, and black. It is a gentle beast with a single fleshy horn unfit for battle and a voice like the chiming of bells. It makes no sound as it walks. Kind to all creatures, it will not step on insects or eat living grass. It is also wise, like the dragon, and is said to carry on its back a document containing the earliest characters of the written Chinese language.

While the phoenix is the emperor of the air, the Ki-Lin is the emperor of the 360 animals of earth. Both of these creatures live in the distant Vermillion Hills, the land of the immortals, where pure streams flow from the K'unlun Mountains. Both are comprised of both male and female, the phoenix of Feng and Whang, the unicorn of Ki and Lin. Like the Feng Huang, the Ki-Lin appears to mankind as a herald of peace, before the reigns of benevolent emperors or the birth of a sage. The animal was first reported in 2697

Chinese unicorn (Ki). (From *Mythical Monsters* by Charles Gould.)

Chinese unicorn (Lin). (From *Mythical Monsters* by Charles Gould.)

B.C., during the reign of Hwang-Ti, and last in the time of the philosopher, Confucius. The Ki-Lin is the best-known of many one-horned animals in ancient Chinese writings.

The Kirin

The Japanese counterpart of the Chinese Ki-Lin, the Kirin is a familiar figure on the packaging of products exported from Japan.

The Karkadan

This ferocious Indian or Persian rhinoceros-like, one-horned monster is so large it can carry off an elephant on its horn. So fierce other animals would not invade its territory, it nonetheless is similar to the Western unicorn in that it can be captured by a young girl, and knife handles made from its horn sweat and tremble when near poison.

The Three-Legged Ass

The unicorn of the ancient Zoroastrians is as large as a mountain. It stands in the middle of the wide ocean. Each of its nine mouths—three in the head, three on its hump, and three on its flanks—is as big as a house. Each of its three feet is as large as a flock of a thousand sheep, and a thousand horsemen could pass between a fetlock and a hoof. It has six sharp eyes: two in the regular position, two on top of the head, and two on the hump. The beast's single horn is hollow gold with a thousand branches spreading out of it.

Gift of the Unicorn

Chinese Folktale

This traditional story from Robert Wyndham's Tales the People Tell in China *links the mysterious and wise Ki-Lin with the honored Chinese sage, Confucius. There is the story that the aging philosopher wept when he came upon a Ki-Lin killed by hunters and saw on its horn a ribbon his own mother had tied there.*

n ancient times, Ki-lin, the fabulous unicorn, appeared occasionally before the emperors. They said the creature was as large as a deer, but it had hoofs like a horse. It had a single horn in the center of its noble head. Its voice was beautiful and as haunting as a monastery bell. And it was so good and gentle that it walked with the greatest care, lest it step upon some living creature. The Ki-lin could neither be captured nor injured by any man. And it appeared only to those emperors who had wisdom and virtue.

When the Middle Kingdom fell into evil ways, and one state warred with another, and kings fought with kings, the unicorn was seen no more. He was seen by no one until the sixth century B.C.

At that time, there lived a woman in the town of Chufu, in the state of Lu, at the base of the sacred mountain Tai Shan. This woman was good and dutiful and truly exceptional. Her one grief was that she had given her husband no son. To be without a son was a great sorrow. If a family had no son, who would worship before the ancestral tablets? With no one to worship, there could be no life after death for the ancestors.

This good woman sorrowed and prayed and begged heaven to take pity upon her and give her a son. Yet no son was born to her.

One day, she decided to make a pilgrimage to a distant temple on the sacred Tai Shan. This temple was thought to be especially holy. There, she planned to appeal to the gods one last time.

As she trudged up the mountain toward the lonely temple, she unknowingly stepped into the secret footprint of the Ki-lin, the gentle unicorn.

At once, the marvelous creature appeared before her, knelt, and dropped a piece of precious jade at her feet. The woman picked up the jade and found these words carved upon the jewel:

"Thy son shall be a ruler without a throne."

When the woman looked up, the unicorn had vanished. But the jade was still in her hand, and she knew that a miracle had taken place.

In time, a son was born to this good woman. He was named Kung Fu Tzu, Confucius. From his earliest days, he showed unusual wisdom, and he became a great teacher. Accompanied by his pupils, he traveled from town to town. All over the land, the people studied and lived by his wise sayings. His influence was as powerful as that of the emperors. Indeed, he ruled without a throne.

From *Tales the People Tell in China* by Robert Wyndham. New York: Julian Messner, 1971, pp. 34-37. Copyright © 1971 by Robert Wyndham.

The Fair Maid and the Snow-White Unicorn

Scottish Folktale

The traditional image of the unicorn with a fair maiden is the starting point for this gentle, magical tale from Winifred Finlay's Folk Tales from Moor and Mountain. *A "besom" is a broom.*

 ong, long ago—when there was still magic in the world and things were not always what they seemed to be—in a ruined castle in the far north of England there dwelt a Fair Maid, with eyes as black as the sloes on the blackthorn in November and skin as white as its blossom in March.

Once, her family had been rich and powerful, owning all the land around as far as the eye could see, and the castle had been in good repair, full of servants to wait on the family and soldiers to protect them from all dangers. Over the years, however, war and misfortune had come upon them, so that all that was left of the once-proud family was the Fair Maid, with eyes as black as the sloes on the blackthorn and skin as white as its blossom, a Maid who went barefoot, and wore patched and faded gowns of silk and velvet.

The little land which had not been sold was overgrown and sadly neglected, providing just enough food for one white cow with red ears, two grey sheep and three speckled hens.

Instead of the many servants to care for the Maid and to look after her, there was only an Old Crone, bent and wrinkled; and instead of the soldiers to guard her, there was only a Unicorn.

He was a splendid creature, as white as the first fall of snow on Muckle Cheviot, the highest of the nearby hills; he resembled a young deer except that, instead of antlers, he had one horn growing from the middle of his velvety forehead, and his eyes, unlike the brown eyes of the deer, were as blue as the speedwell which grew in the castle moat.

As the years passed, travellers began to talk of having caught a glimpse of this Maid who wandered barefoot over the lonely hills, and who was accompanied everywhere by a snow-white Unicorn: hearing this, the young men in the land thought to themselves what fine sport it would be to hunt such a rare creature and to kill it, and then to woo the Fair Maid and marry her.

Through the green valleys and over the heather-clad hills they journeyed, until they came within sight of the ruined castle, and there they hid themselves behind clumps of trees or great boulders, and waited.

When at the last the Maid appeared with her snow-white Unicorn, each man prepared to draw his bowstring, thinking that never had he hunted a finer beast, or wooed a fairer maid; but, at the very moment that the hunters were about to let fly their deadly, goose-feathered arrows, the Unicorn shook his head, so that each huntsman felt as though he had been turned to stone, and helpless and speechless he remained until maid and beast had passed out of sight.

"Who wants to hunt a unicorn in these bleak hills?" the young men cried angrily, when they returned to their homes. "As for the Maid, she dresses like a beggar and is far from beautiful. No man in his senses would dream of wooing her." And not one of them admitted how helpless he had been when the Unicorn had shaken its head.

So the word was spread that the Maid was both poor and ugly, and the Unicorn not worth the hunting. Soon people forgot all about them, and the Maid dwelt happily in her ruined castle with the Old Crone, and roamed the hills and valleys with the Unicorn by her side.

Now it happened that one fine, spring morning the Maid and Unicorn wandered farther afield than usual, climbing right over Muckle Cheviot itself and down into a valley where the banks were ablaze with the golden flowers of the bonnie broom, and where, in the distance, a grey stone farmhouse huddled against the steep hillside.

"What sound is that?" the Maid cried, halting suddenly and looking around her.

"It is only the feet of the wind in the bonnie broom," the Unicorn answered.

"It is that, and it is more than that," the Maid said. "It is the sad, soft cry of those who have been rejected, and it breaks my heart to hear it. Who are you?" she called out. "Why do you weep so bitterly?"

At that, a little man, old and bearded, and wrinkled, stepped from under the bonnie broom beside her.

"We are the Little People, Fair Maid," he said, "and we weep because we have nowhere to go. Ever since yonder farm was built, I, who am the Oldest and Wisest, have lived there with my people—with my children, and my grandchildren, and my great-grandchildren.

"This spring, a new farmer moved in, and his wife says she has no time for the Little People, no butter to spare for our bread, no milk to give us for our babies. She swept us all out with a heather besom, then locked and bolted the door; and now my people weep because they are frightened and hungry and homeless."

"My castle has long lacked a roof," the Maid said. "The wind sighs o' nights and whistles along the passages, and the rain drives through the windows, but the kitchen is snug and warm. If the Old Crone and the Unicorn are willing, you may share it with us and live there as long as you please."

"I am willing," the Unicorn said.

"I am willing," the Old Crone muttered, when the Maid returned to her castle with the Little People clustering anxiously about her. And she skimmed some of the cream from the basin beside her, and set it down on the hearth for the Little People, and cut a thick crust off the loaf she had just baked, and set it beside the cream.

"You shall have no cause to regret this day," said the Oldest and Wisest to the Maid.

"You shall have no cause to regret this day," his people agreed. After they had drunk the cream and eaten the bread, the women and children set up their tables, chairs, cooking pots and all their possessions on the left-hand side of the great fireplace, while the men scurried about the ruined castle, probing and rapping and banging, nodding their heads and stroking their beards, their eyes gleaming with excitement.

That night, while the Maid slept soundly on the right-hand side of the kitchen fireplace, with the Unicorn at her feet, and the Old Crone stretched out on a settle, the castle was filled with the sound of singing and whistling, with the buzz of little saws and the tap of tiny hammers. When the Maid awoke the next morning, she found, to her surprise, that a new roof covered the castle and that no longer could the wind enter at will.

All the next night the Little People worked, and when the Maid awoke on the second morning, she found, to her amazement, that the doors had been renewed, and glass put in the windows, so that no longer could the rain and snow enter at will.

While the Maid slept on the third night, the Little People worked harder than ever before; and when she awoke on the third morning, she found, to her astonishment, all the rooms furnished and restored as they had been when the family was rich and powerful. The walls were hung with tapestries, the beds furnished with warm coverings, while the long table in the great Hall was set with goblets of Venetian glass and dishes of the finest silver.

"Now there is no need for us to live in the kitchen," the Oldest and Wisest said. "If you are willing, we shall make our home henceforward in the room at the top of the west tower."

"I am willing," the Maid said. "But I must ask the Unicorn and the Old Crone too."

"We are willing," answered the Unicorn and the Old Crone.

That night, for the first time in her life, the Maid slept in the big four-poster bed in the Great Bedroom. When she awoke the next morning and looked out of the window, she found to her delight that the fields had been ploughed and sown and harrowed, and that where there had been one white cow with red ears, now there were a hundred; where there had been two grey sheep, now there were two hundred, and instead of three speckled hens, now there were three hundred.

"How ever can I thank you for all you have done for me?" she asked the Oldest and Wisest.

"By accepting one last word of advice," he answered. "Your castle is repaired, your lands cultivated and your flocks and herds thriving. All that is lacking is a husband for you and a master for the castle."

"A master," the Old Crone agreed.

"A husband," the Unicorn whispered, with a strange look in his blue, blue eyes.

"Very well," the Maid said. "How shall I set about finding a husband for myself and a master for the castle?"

"Leave that to me," answered the Oldest and Wisest. "I shall bid the birds spread the news that suitors for your hand may present themselves here on the first morning of May."

Joyfully the birds spread the news that, in her castle in the lonely hills, the Maid awaited her suitors, so that from the Frozen North and the Warm South, from the Eastern Seaboard and the Western Isles, the princes journeyed forth.

The first to arrive was the Prince of the Frozen North, a handsome warrior, who talked of battles and the joyful sound of steel against steel in hand-to-hand fights. Never, the Maid thought, had she met such a brave and handsome prince—which was not surprising, as he was the first man she had ever spoken to.

"I shall marry you," she said, "if you can give me the right answer to one question. Would you have room in your castle for the Little People?"

"The Little People?" the prince cried. "Why, they were all killed a long time ago, and a good thing too, for all they did was interfere and cause trouble."

"You are not the husband for me, nor the master for this castle," the Maid declared, and the Prince of the Frozen North departed in anger, while the Unicorn sighed softly.

The second to arrive was the Prince of the Warm South, a handsome huntsman, who talked of the thrill of chasing deer and hares, and the joyful sound of the horn in the green woods. Never, the Maid thought, had she met such a splendid and handsome prince—which was not surprising, as he was only the second man she had ever spoken to.

"I shall marry you," she said, "if you can give me the right answer to one question. Would you have room in your castle for the Little People?"

"The Little People?" the prince cried. "Why, they were chased away from this country years ago, and a good thing too, for all they did was make a nuisance of themselves."

"Then you are not the husband for me, nor the master for this castle," the Maid declared, and the Prince of the Warm South departed in anger, and again the Unicorn sighed softly.

The third to arrive was the Prince of the Eastern Seaboard, a handsome sailor who talked of storms and shipwrecks, and the joyful sound of the sea surging on the sandy shore. Never, the Maid thought, had she met such a valiant and handsome prince—which was not surprising, as he was only the third man she had ever spoken to.

"I shall marry you," she said, "if you can give me the right answer to one question. Would you have room in your castle for the Little People?"

"The Little People?" the prince cried. "Why, they were all drowned years ago, and good riddance to bad rubbish, say I."

"Then you are not the husband for me, nor the master for this castle," the Maid declared, and the Prince of the Eastern Seaboard departed in anger, while the Unicorn sighed hopefully.

The fourth and last to arrive was the Prince of the Western Isles, a handsome musician, who sang sweetly to the accompaniment of his harp, of the magic of old, half-forgotten days. Never, the Maid thought, had she met such an accomplished and handsome prince—which was not surprising, as he was only the fourth man she had ever spoken to.

"I shall marry you," she said, "if you can give me the right answer to one question. Would you have room in your castle for the Little People?"

"The Little People?" the prince cried. "Why, they do not exist and they never did. They were created by story-tellers, poets and musicians like me, and without us, they have no life of their own."

"Then you are not the husband for me, nor the master for this castle," the Maid declared, and the Prince of the Western Isles departed in anger, while the Unicorn watched, but made never a sound.

"They were all brave and handsome young men, Oldest and Wisest," the Maid said, "but not one of them would have allowed you and your people to stay here as I promised. What shall I do now?"

"Follow your heart," the Old Crone snapped, before the Oldest and Wisest could answer.

The Maid thought for a moment, and then turned to the Unicorn.

"If you were a prince, would you have room in your castle for the Little People?" she asked.

"Always," the Unicorn answered.

"Then I shall marry you because, ever since I can remember, you have looked after me, and been good and kind to me, and also because you love the Little People as I do," the Maid declared.

Because all this happened long, long ago—when there was still magic in the world, and things were not always what they seemed to be—the snow-white Unicorn sighed again. And disappeared.

And in his place there stood a prince who was braver, and more handsome, and much, much wiser than any of the four suitors who had journeyed to woo the Maid on that May morning.

So the Maid and the Unicorn-Prince were married, and they, and the Old Crone, and all the Little People with their leader, the Oldest and Wisest, lived happily and prosperously ever after.

From *Folk Tales for Moor and Mountain* by Winifred Finlay. New York: Roy, 1969, pp. 66-73.

The Unicorn Today

In 1827, science struck what seemed to be the final blow to the reality of the unicorn. The French naturalist Georges Cuvier declared no cloven-hoofed animal could have a single horn. Such animals, he said, had a divided frontal bone and that one horn could not grow from the middle of it. The rhinoceros did not count because its horn was made of bristles, not bone.

But the slain unicorn returns to life in the final tapestry in the *Hunt of the Unicorn* series, and so it returned again, after Cuvier proved it impossible. For centuries, travelers had related tales of the unicorn, and those tales continued. In the mid-1800s, the Abbe Huc wrote, "The unicorn really exists in Thibet." There it had the names of *serou* and *tesopo*, and *kere* in Mongolia. The unicorn was commonly reported seen in Africa, where it was variously known as *a'nasa* and *ndzoodzoo*.

In 1933, a Maine doctor, W. Franklin Dove, artificially created a unicorn. He knew what Georges Cuvier had said about single horns, but he disagreed. Maintaining that horns grew *into*, not *out of* the skull, Dr. Dove transplanted the horn buds of a day-old calf from the sides to the front of its skull, touching above the bone division. The horn buds grew together into a single horn, just as the doctor predicted they would.

There are reports that sheep of Nepal were artificially made into unicorns. Also, some say that for centuries certain tribes of herders in Africa have transplanted the horn buds of their cattle so that single horns would mark the leaders of their herds. If this practice is as old as some say, some of the travelers' tales through the ages might actually be true.

The Unicorn

Ringling Brothers and Barnum & Bailey featured unicornized goats in their circus, but dropped the acts in response to the protests of animal rights groups. A current unicorn issue is the poaching and selling of the parts of the endangered rhinoceros, particularly the one-horned Indian rhino (*Rhinoceros unicornis*). Since ancient times, some groups have believed that rhinoceros horn, like the alicorn of the rhino's mythical counterpart, has medicinal value. Illegal hunting of the endangered animals has been condemned by the international community.

As for the legendary unicorn, the marvelous beast has followed the pattern of other animals now considered to be fantastic. After the development of modern science in the 1600s, it wandered away from mankind for about two hundred years.

While African explorers were still searching for actual unicorns, Lewis Carroll gave the unicorn comic treatment, as he had done with the griffin. In *Through the Looking Glass*, Alice comes upon the Lion and the Unicorn, fist-fighting for the crown. Alice and the Unicorn each thinks the other is a fabulous monster. The Unicorn says to Alice, "if you'll believe in me, I'll believe in you," and Alice serves plum cake to the two combatants.

The Unicorn has since charmed readers in scores of children's stories and poems and in fantasy novels. Books are only one mark of the immense popularity the magical creature now enjoys. On tee-shirts and calendars, in porcelain and plastic, the unicorn is everywhere, sometimes cute and cuddly, sometimes noble. This mystical, solitary animal may be less than comfortable with the commercial attention it is now receiving, but after eluding alicorn hunters, scholars, and explorers, the unicorn will be with us for ages to come.

The African Unicorn

W. Winwood Reade

In his 1864 book, Savage Africa, *British explorer W. Winwood Reade summarized the many sightings of the elusive unicorn, right up to his own time. More recent discoveries of artificial unicornization seem to indicate that some of the accounts could have been true. Persepolis was the ancient capital of Persia. A "jennet" is a small horse.*

 t must be laid down as a certain principle that man can originate nothing; that lies are always truths embellished, distorted, or turned inside out. There are other facts besides those which lie on the surface, and it is the duty of the traveler and historian to sift and wash the gold-grains of truth from the dirt of fable.

* * *

Of all animals which have been classed as fabulous, the unicorn is the most remarkable, since to this very day it is impossible for a careful writer to make a positive assertion respecting its existence.

The ancients compared their *monoceros* to a horse with a stag's head, which proves that they had seen an animal very different from the rhinoceros. They also distinctly name the *unicorn-ass*, an animal of great size, swift of foot, solitary in his habits, and having a horn striped with white, black, and brown.

Garcias, a writer of the sixteenth century, relates that the Portuguese navigators saw, between the Cape of Good Hope and Cape Corrientes, an animal having the head and mane of a horse, with one movable horn. In this same region Sparmann and Barrow saw representations of a one-horned animal. The rocks of Camdebo and Bambo are covered with them—a curious fact, setting zoology aside; for it proves the ancient connection of Caffraria with Asia; the unicorn, among the Persians and Hebrews, being the symbol of kingly power. It is with this meaning delineated on the monuments of Persepolis, and on the royal arms of Great Britain.

* * *

The next authority is that of a Portuguese who had lived some time in Abyssinia, and is quoted by Father Tellez.

"It is certain that the unicorn is not to be confounded with the *abada*, about which they usually dispute; this one may see by the difference of their names, as well as by the difference of their body and parts, and it would appear by the *abada* which we have seen and by the unicorn which we have seen painted. The latter has a long straight horn of admirable virtue; the *abada* has two crooked horns, which are not so sovereign, although they will serve as antidotes against poison. The country of the unicorn, which is an animal of Africa, where only it is known, is the province of Agoa, in the kingdom of Damotes, although it is occasionally seen in more distant places. This animal is as large as a fine horse, is a dark bay color, the mane and tail black, short, and thin, though in other parts of the province observed to be longer and thicker. On the forehead there is a beautiful horn five palms long, as they are usually painted, the color being nearly white. They live in woods and retired thickets, sometimes coming out onto the plains, where they are not often seen, because they are timid animals, not numerous, and easily hidden in the wood. . . .

"A Portuguese captain, a man of years and good credit, and held in great esteem by the princes of this empire, under whom he serves, told me this story about unicorns. He said that once, as he was returning from the army with twenty other Portuguese soldiers, and they were resting one morning in a little valley encircled by very thick trees, getting ready their breakfast while their horses grazed on the rich pasture, scarcely were they seated when there sprang out of the thickest part of the wood a beautiful horse of the same shape and color that I have described. He came so rapidly that he did not observe the people till he was quite among them; then he was startled, began to tremble, and suddenly bounded back, leaving, however, sufficient time to the spectators to see and observe him with pleasure. The knowledge which I have of this captain induces me to relate this as an undoubted fact.

"In another part of the same province, where it is stony and mountainous, people have often seen this animal feeding among several others of different kinds. This is the most remote part of the province; that is why exiles are usually sent there by the emperor. It is bounded by high mountains, below which are vast plains and forests inhabited by various kinds of wild beasts. To this place a tyrannical emperor named Adamas-Segued sent without cause several Portuguese, who, from the tops of the mountains, saw the unicorn feeding in the plains below, the distance not being so great but that they could observe distinctly that it was like a fine Spanish jennet, having a horn in his forehead.

"These testimonies, especially that of the good old man, John Gabriel, with what the missionary, my companion, affirmed also of his own knowledge, confirm me in the belief that this celebrated animal is found in the province, and that young ones are born and bred there."

The latest traveler who has spoken of the unicorn is Dr. Baikie, who, when I was in Africa, had started on an incursion after this animal, the existence of which he must therefore have credited, and could only have done so upon reliable authority. That such an animal has existed, there can, I think be little doubt.

From *Savage Africa* by W. Winwood Reade. New York: Harper and Brothers, 1864, pp. 369, 372-75.

The Last Unicorns

Edward D. Hoch

For centuries, scholars who would deny the existence of the unicorn pointed out that if the animal had actually lived, it would have been listed as one that boarded Noah's ark before the great Flood. Therefore, they concluded, because the unicorn was not so named, there was obviously no such animal. This modern fantasy by Edward D. Hoch finds a way around that scholarly conclusion.

he rain was still falling by the time he reached the little wooden shack that stood in the center of the green, fertile valley. He opened his cloak for an instant to knock at the door, not really expecting a reply.

But it opened, pulled over the roughness of the rock floor by great hairy hands. "Come in," a voice commanded him. "Hurry! Before this rain floods me out."

"Thank you," the traveler said, removing the soggy garment that had covered him and squeezing out some of the water. "It's good to find a dry place. I've come a long way."

"Not many people are about in this weather," the man told him, pulling at his beard with a quick, nervous gesture.

"I came looking for you."

"For me? What is your name?"

"You can call me Shem. I come from beyond the mountains."

The bearded man grunted. "I don't know the name. What do you seek?"

Shem sat down to rest himself on a pale stone seat. "I hear talk that you have two fine unicorns here, recently brought from Africa."

The man smiled proudly. "That is correct. The only such creatures in this part of the world. I intend to breed them and sell them to the farmers as beasts of burden."

"Oh?"

"They can do the work of strong horses and at the same time use their horn to defend themselves against attack."

"True," Shem agreed. "Very true. I . . . I don't suppose you'd want to part with them . . . ?"

"Part with them! Are you mad, man? It cost me money to bring them all the way from Africa!"

"How much would you take for them?"

The bearded man rose from his seat. "No amount, ever! Come back in two years when I've bred some. Until then, begone with you!"

"I *must* have them, sir."

"You *must* have nothing! Begone from here now before I take a club to you!" And with those words he took a menacing step forward.

Shem retreated out the door, back into the rain, skipping lightly over a rushing stream of water from the higher ground. The door closed on him, and he was alone. But he looked out into the fields, where a small, barnlike structure stood glistening in the downpour.

They would be in there, he knew.

He made his way across the field, sometimes sinking to his ankles in puddles of muddy water. But finally he reached the outbuilding and went in through a worn, rotten door.

Yes, they were there . . . Two tall and handsome beasts, very much like horses, but with longer tails and with that gleaming, twisted horn shooting straight up from the center of their foreheads. Unicorns—one of the rarest of God's creatures.

He moved a bit closer, trying now to lure them out of the building without startling them. But there was a noise, and he turned suddenly to see the bearded man standing there, a long staff upraised in his hands.

"You try to steal them," he shouted, lunging forward.

The staff thudded against the wall, inches from Shem's head. "Listen, old man . . ."

"Die! Die, you robber!"

But Shem leaped to one side, around the bearded figure of wrath, and through the open doorway. Behind him, the unicorns gave a fearful snort and trampled the earthen floor with their hoofs.

Shem kept running, away from the shack, away from the man with the staff, away from the fertile valley.

After several hours of plodding over the rain-swept hills, he came at last upon his father's village, and he went down among the houses to the place where the handful of people had gathered.

And he saw his father standing near the base of the great wooden vessel, and he went up to him sadly.

"Yes, my son?" the old man questioned, unrolling a long damp scroll of parchment.

"No unicorns, Father."

"No unicorns," Noah repeated sadly, scratching out the name on his list. "It is too bad. They were handsome beasts . . ."

From "The Last Unicorns" by Edward D. Hoch. From *100 Great Fantasy Short Short Stories*, 1984. Copyright © 1958 by Columbia Publications, Inc. Renewed by the author.

The Unicorn

The Dragon

 ong after dinosaurs passed into the earth, the dragon uncoiled in the cave of the human mind.

In the West, the dragon slithered up from the foundations of the world, shaking mountains as it came, and emerged as a great scaly serpent, its eyes shining with wisdom and evil. It wrestled with gods and tempted humans with the gift of knowledge. It grew legs and spiny wings and thrashed a barbed tail. It breathed fire and soared in the windy darkness. It captured maidens, guarded treasure, and battled knights to the death. Among the fiery legions of the Devil, it engorged sinners. It stalked the righteous, roaring at the edge of dream.

In the East, the dragon unfolded from the earth in the spring of the year and ascended to the sky. The grandest of creatures, its nine forms were those of animals of earth, sea, and sky. Long whiskers curled from its muzzle, and under its bearded chin glowed a pearl of great power. Its breath formed clouds and rain; its swirling movement created wind, lightning, and thunder. Others of its race spread through other regions of the world, some to build palaces in the sea, others to direct the rivers and the streams, to guard treasure in the earth, to rule the quadrants of the sky, to reside in the upper heavens. The dragon of the East, seen as a protector and benefactor of humankind, is honored as the embodiment of wisdom, strength, and good fortune.

King of the wonder beasts, the dragon has roamed the world since the beginnings of the human imagination, changing form and character through time and place, from nightmare monster to awesome force of nature.

The Dragon from the Past

In ancient Greek and Latin, "drakon" and "draco" simply meant "serpent." They were also related to terms such as "sharp-sighted" and "watchful." The English term for dragon, "drake," as in "firedrake," also comes from the Greek word. "Worm" is an archaic word for serpent, snake, or dragon.

The Constellation Draco

A meeting point for many of the older dragon myths is the circumpolar constellation Draco, "the Dragon." It winds across the northern sky, from its tail between the Great and Little Bears to its head, with its two bright eyes, under the foot of Hercules. The constellation has been identified with dragons from the Babylonian Tiamat to the Norse Midgard Serpent. The Dragon winds its way through all the stories, encircling the world, coiling in trees, guarding treasure, and fighting heroes and gods to the death.

According to *Enuma Elish*, the Babylonian epic of creation, Tiamat, the mother of the gods, had a serpent-like body with hide so tough it could not be pierced by weapons. She and Apsu, both born of water, were the first two gods. They mated and bore other gods, so many other gods that Apsu became annoyed with them and wanted to destroy them. When the younger gods learned of this, they killed Apsu. Tiamat then battled the gods who were responsible for Apsu's death. These opposing gods selected Marduk to challenge the vengeful goddess, Tiamat. Marduk armed himself with bow and arrows and a net of winds and drove to the terrifying goddess in the chariot of a tempest. When Tiamat opened her mouth to swallow him, he loosed the winds into her and shot an arrow directly into her heart. Marduk, the first dragon slayer, then cut Tiamat in half. One half of her body became earth, the other half sky.

In another battle of the gods, the Greek god, Zeus, led his Olympians against the older, monstrous Titans. At the height of the fighting, the goddess Athena seized the Titanic dragon by the tail and threw it into the void. The spinning serpent tangled among the stars, where it remains to this day as the constellation Draco.

The head of Draco lies under the foot of the constellation Hercules. No stranger to grappling with serpents, Hercules was only a baby when he first displayed his strength by strangling two snakes a goddess had sent to attack him. Also, the hero had already lopped off the heads of the Hydra of Lerna by the time he set out on one of his last labors, to bring back to King Eurystheus the immortal Golden Apples that grew in the Garden of the Hesperides. The tree was guarded by the dragon, Ladon. Like the hero Jason, who killed the dragon that guarded the Golden Fleece, Hercules slew the serpent to reach the treasure. Ever after, Hercules carried a shield bearing the coiled likeness of the beast.

Draco is also associated with the adventures of Cadmus, the founder of Thebes. Dragons first entered his story when he consulted the Oracle at Delphi, where the god Apollo had battled and killed the great serpent, Python. While following the instructions of the Oracle, Cadmus killed the dragon guarding a spring near the site of the city he was fated to build. The goddess Athena ordered Cadmus to sow the teeth of the dragon like seeds. When he did as she demanded, the teeth sprouted into warriors who fought each other until only five remained. Those five pledged themselves to Cadmus's service.

Athena kept some of the teeth and later gave them to Jason during his quest for the Golden Fleece.

In Norse mythology, the Midgard Serpent lay coiled around the Sacred Ash, gnawing at its roots, until the god Odin seized it and hurled it into the darkness, where it encircled the world and now twists among the stars.

Early Western astronomers also referred to Draco as the Old Serpent, the snake that tempted Eve in the Garden of Eden.

Also in the northern sky is a group of constellations representing another well-known classical tale of a monster many called a sea serpent or a dragon. The hero Perseus slew the sea serpent Cetus to rescue Andromeda, the daughter of King Cepheus and Queen Cassiopeia. All of the characters from this myth, including the monster Cetus, are to be found in the stars.

As the old stories show, the Western dragon was originally a great serpent. In the natural histories, too, the dragon was a large snake. Traditionally a natural enemy of the elephant, the serpent was said to coil itself around its mammoth prey and constrict it until the elephant collapsed, killing them both. In snake lore, the creatures often had crests, beards, teeth, and hypnotic eyes, and their heads were filled with precious gems.

The Monster of the Middle Ages

While the ancient dragon of the West was often wise as well as violent, associated with oracles and the gods, the beast changed over centuries into a monster that was pure evil.

In the bestiaries, the beast is similar to that of the ancient reptile. It is a crested serpent that attacks and kills elephants, and it is identified with the Devil. In the Bible, the Old Serpent first appears in the Garden of Eden, leading to the Fall, and later in the book of Revelation it is a "great red dragon, having seven heads and ten horns, and seven crowns upon his heads." Michael and his angels battle the demon in Heaven and cast it down to earth. In nightmarish medieval paintings, the gaping mouth of the dragon becomes the gate of Hell.

The Archangel Michael's battle with the dragon was one of the most popular subjects of the art of the Middle Ages. Another dragon slayer celebrated in picture and story was St. George. As one of the stories goes, George's travels took him one day to the Libyan town of Silena, on the shore of a vast lake. There he came upon a young girl tied to a stake. When he asked her why she was there, she told him about the monster that lived in the lake. To keep it from destroying the town, the people had offered it two sheep a day, then one sheep and a man or woman. After the demon had devoured all the other young people of the town, it fell to her father, the king, to sacrifice her, his only child. While George listened to the girl's tale, the monster emerged from the waters beside them. George pierced the beast with his lance, defeating but not killing it. He unbound the girl and had her tie her belt around the monster's throat. She led the creature into the town, and it was killed in the city square. George, a latter-day Perseus, became the patron saint of England.

The dragon played a major role in the art and heroic poetry of Northern Europe. Wooden serpents intertwined in decorative carvings. The ships of the Vikings had carved dragonhead prows and sterns that ended in curling tails. After having killed the monster Grendel and his mother, the aging Anglo-Saxon hero Beowulf battled the dragon guarding a treasure, and the two killed each other. And the young German hero, Siegfried, with a sword forged in the underground home of the dwarfs, slew the deadly dragon Fafnir, guardian of the treasure hoard of an ancient race. Tasting the blood of the beast gave Siegfried the power to understand the language of birds.

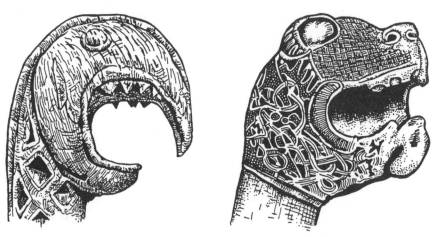

Viking longship prows.

Heraldic Dragons

The evil monster of the medieval stories became a noble and courageous figure in heraldry. The beginnings of the heraldic dragon were emblems on ancient shields and banners and the dragon-shaped windsock standards of Roman armies. Uther Pendragon, the father of the legendary King Arthur, used the figure because he had a vision of a dragon flaming in the sky. "Pendragon" means "head dragon," or chieftain. The dragon image was handed down to Arthur, and became the battle standard of British kings.

Heraldic four-legged dragon.

The heraldic dragon has the toothed jaws and scaly stomach of a crocodile, pointed ears, the talons of an eagle, the ribbed wings of a bat, and a serpentine tail. Both its tongue and tail are often barbed. A well-known representation of this beast is the red dragon of Wales. The wyvern is the two-legged variety of the four-legged dragon, and the cockatrice (basilisk) is similar to the wyvern except it has the head of a rooster rather than that of a dragon.

Here Be Dragons

"Here Be Dragons" was a phrase sometimes used on the edges of old maps, referring to remote, unexplored areas and the oceans at the rims of the earth (see the map on page xviii). It's clear from the Western dragon's history that "here" was many places and many forms. The great beast encircled the earth and wound through the heavens. It lived in myth and legend, in art, in bestiaries and in heraldry, and it even entered the Renaissance natural histories. In those serious zoological books, the dragon enjoyed one more period of credibility before it moved on to yet another stage of its long and varied life.

Heraldic wyvern.

Heraldic cockatrice.

Perseus and Andromeda

Ovid

In this ancient myth, Perseus has just killed the snake-haired gorgon, Medusa. As he flies towards home with winged shoes, still carrying her head, he sees a girl chained to a rock on the shore below. Queen Cassiopeia had offended a sea god, who sent a monster, Cetus, to devour her lands. King Cepheus was told the only way to save the kingdom was to offer their daughter, Andromeda, to the sea beast. So, that is what he did.

Ammon is the king of the Egyptian gods; Jove is the king of the Roman gods (equivalent of the Greek god, Zeus); Hymen and Cupid are the Roman gods of marriage and love.

erseus clipped wings to heels and buckled on the curved
Sword that he carried and as quickly leaped,
Sailing at ease full speed through cloudless air.
He travelled over countless multitudes
Until he saw Egyptian shore below him
Where Cepheus was king, where unjust Ammon
Had ordered Andromeda to be punished
Because the poor girl had a foolish mother
Who talked too much. When Perseus saw her
Fastened to a rock, arms chained above the sea,
But for hot tears that rippled down her face
And swaying hair that fluttered in the wind,
He might have thought the girl a work of art,
Carved out of stone. Dazed by the sight of her
Fire was lightning in his veins; he could not speak;
Lost as he gazed he almost failed to beat his wings,
Then, as he landed near the girl, remarked,
"O, you should never wear the chains that hold you;
Wear those that lovers cherish as they sleep
In one another's arms. Tell me your name,
Why you are here, the place where you were born."
At first she did not answer, being modest;
She feared to talk to any bold young man,
And if her hands had not been chained behind her
She would have hid her face. Meanwhile her eyes,
Though free to speak, rained down her ceaseless tears.

Then, as he pressed her, to prevent his thinking
That she was guilty of some hopeless crime
She softly said her name, told who she was,
And how her mother bragged of her own beauty.
And as she spoke huge noises lashed the air,
Roaring from waves where a great dragon floated,
Riding the sea, and as it clambered toward her
The girl screamed while her parents, wild and harried,
Raced to her side, and though they beat their breasts,
Weeping their helpless tears, they knew her danger
And clung to her, while the young stranger said,
"There will be time for weeping afterward,
Yet time for rescue is a little space:
If I took to this girl as Perseus,
Jove's son and son of her who in a cell
Received Jove's favor in that golden rain
That filled her veins with life, if you will take me
As one who killed the snake-haired Gorgoness,
As Perseus who rides the air with wings,
You should be flattered by your daughter's prospects—
A worthy husband as your son-in-law.
With the gods' grace, I'll add to my distinctions
By helping you, and if your daughter's life
Is saved, she's mine." The parents took his terms
(As who would not?) and pleaded for the rescue;
And promised him rich lands as daughter's dowry.

Look out to sea! Swift as a diving, tossing,
Knife-sharp-nosed ship that cuts the waves, propelled
By sweat-soaked arms of galley slaves, the dragon
Sailed up while churning waters at its breast
Broke into spray, leeside and windward; plunging
It came as near to shore as a Balearic
Sling could send its shot. Perseus, leaping
From earth behind him, vaulted to mid-air;
The dragon saw his shadow on the sea
And plunged to tear at it. Then, as Jove's eagle,
When he has found a snake in a broad meadow
Turning its mottled body to the sun,
Falls on the unseeing creature from the air,

Perseus and Andromeda   111

And as the bird, knowing the snake's forked tongue,
Grips its scaled neck and sinks his claws within it,
So Perseus dove upon the raging dragon,
Thrusting, hilt-deep, the sword into its shoulder.
Burning with its gaped wound, the dragon reared
Its bulk in air, then dived, veered like a boar
When it has been surrounded by quick hounds,
Loud with the kill. Perseus, dodging, swayed
Past snapping jaws on agile, dancing wings;
Then as the beast rolled its soft belly open,
Or bared its neck, his crooked sword struck in:
At back grown tough with sea-wet barnacles,
At flanks, or at the thin and fishlike tail.
The beast began to vomit purple spew,
And Perseus' wings, damp with salt spray, grew heavy;
He saw a rock that pierced the shifting waters
As they stilled, now curtained by the riding
Of the waves, and leaped to safety on it.
With left hand grasping on a ledge of cliff
He struck his sword three times and then again
Into the dragon's bowels. Then all the shores,
Even the highest balconies of heaven,
From which the gods looked down on Perseus,
Rang with great cheers; Cepheus and his wife,
Cassiope, called to their hero as a gallant
Bridegroom who saved the glory of their house.

* * *

He took his Andromeda as his bride.
Hymen and Cupid shook the wedding torch;
The fires were lit and incense filled the air,
And through the streets houses were hung with garlands;
Behind each gate and lintel, song echoed to the flute,
All music of the joy that shone within.
Then great doors of the palace were thrown back
Where golden rooms showed gentles to a feast
And Cepheus' court joined in a celebration.

From *The Metamorphoses* by Ovid. Translated by Horace Gregory. New York:
Viking, 1958, pp. 131-34.

The Dragon

A Dragon Hunt

Philostratus

The monstrous fire-breathing drake from medieval legend is only one of innumerable shapes the dragon has taken on through its long life. To ancient writers like Philostratus [Phil-AH-struh-tus], A.D. 170-245, dragons were large serpents with fabulous attributes. In his Life of Apollonius of Tyana, *Philostratus presents the mysterious beasts as earth-shaking creatures with jeweled eyes. "Congener" means one of the same kind.*

he whole of India is girt with dragons of enormous size; for not only the marshes are full of them, but the mountains as well, and there is not a single ridge without one. Now the marsh kind are sluggish in their habits and are thirty cubits long, and they have no crest standing up on their heads, but in this respect resemble the she-dragons. Their backs however are very black, with fewer scales on them than the other kinds; and Homer has described them with deeper insight than have most poets, for he says that the dragon that lived hard by the spring in Aulis had a tawny back; but other poets declare that the congener of this one in the grove of Nemea also had a crest, a feature which we could not verify in regard to the marsh dragons.

And the dragons along the foothills and the mountain crests make their way into the plains after their quarry, and get the better all round of those in the marshes; for indeed they reach a greater length, and move faster than the swiftest rivers, so that nothing escapes them. These actually have a crest, of moderate extent and height when they are young; but as they reach their full size, it grows with them and extends to a considerable height, at which time also they turn red and get serrated backs. This kind also have beards, and lift their necks on high, while their scales glitter like silver; and the pupils of their eyes consist of a fiery stone, and they say that this has an uncanny power for many secret purposes. The plain specimen is a real prize of the hunters whenever it draws into its folds an elephant; for the destruction of both creatures is the result, and those who capture the dragons are rewarded by getting the eyes and skin and teeth. In most respects the tusks resemble the largest swine's, but they are slighter in build and twisted, and have a point as unabraded as sharks' teeth.

Now the dragons of the mountains have scales of a golden colour, and in length excel those of the plain, and they have bushy beards, which also are of a golden hue; and their eyebrows are more prominent than those of the plain, and their eye is sunk deep under the eyebrow, and emits a terrible and ruthless glance. And they give off a noise like the clashing of brass whenever they are burrowing under the earth, and from their crests, which are all fiery red, there flashes a fire brighter than a torch. They also can catch the elephants, though they are themselves caught by the Indians in the following manner. They embroider golden runes on a scarlet cloak, which they lay in front of the animal's burrow after charming the runes to cause sleep; for this is the only way to overcome the eyes of the dragon, which are otherwise inflexible, and much mysterious lore is sung by them to overcome him. These runes induce the dragon to stretch his neck out of his burrow and fall asleep over them; then the Indians fall upon him as he lies there, and despatch him with blows of their axes, and having cut off the head they despoil it of its gems. And they say that in the heads of the mountain dragons there are stored away stones of flowery colour, which flash out all kinds of hues, and possess a mystical power such as resided in the ring, which they say belonged to Gyges. But often the Indian, in spite of his axe and his cunning, is caught by the dragon, who carries him off into his burrow, and almost shakes the mountains as he disappears. These are also said to inhabit the mountains in the neighborhood of the Red Sea, and they say that they hear them hissing terribly and that they see them go down to the shore and swim far out into the sea. It was impossible however to ascertain the number of years that this creature lives, nor would my statements be believed. This is all I know about dragons.

From *Life of Apollonius of Tyana* by Philostratus. Translated by F. C. Conybeare. Cambridge, Mass.: Harvard University Press, 1960, pp. 243-47.

Beowulf's Dragon Fight

Old English Epic

One of the greatest accounts of a knight battling a dragon is in the Old English heroic poem, Beowulf (eighth century). Renowned for slaying the monster Grendel and its mother, Beowulf is an aging warrior-king when a dragon whose treasure-hoard had been violated destroys the countryside with its fiery breath. To rid his kingdom of the beast, Beowulf dresses in battle gear a final time and ventures to the dragon's den. In this segment, Beowulf is nearly overcome with heat and exhaustion when his relative Wiglaf comes to his aid. Both the dragon and Beowulf die from their wounds.

"Worm" is a Germanic word for dragon, "brynie" is a chain-mail shirt, and "board" a shield. "Naegling" is the sword of Beowulf, king of the "Weders" (Geats). A "thane" is a land-holding subject.

 his was the first time
For young Wiglaf, that he should join
The rush of war with his dear lord. His mind
Did not melt, nor his legacy of strength
Go weak in the fight, as the worm found out,
After they had come together.

* * *

Wiglaf waded through the reek with keen-headed
Help for his lord—with golden words and few.
"Dear Beowulf, live up to all you have done,
As in your youth you said you would never
As long as you had life let right fame
Fall away. Now, long famous for your deeds,
Pure prince, you must with all your might
Serve your worthy life well—I will help!"

At these words, the worm came angrily on,
For a second time, a foul gust of hate,
Worm-infested fire, most loathsome of men,
To fall upon his foes. Waves of fire burned
Shield to rim. A scorching byrnie could not
Yield much help for the young spear-warrior,
But the youth under his kinsman's cover
Went strong in arm, when his own board was
Reduced to flaming dust. Then the captain
King's mind took fame in hand, struck so hard
With his blade of war, that between his hand
And that hateful head shattered Naegling stood,
Went weak in the fight, Beowulf's own sword,
Old-etched in gray! Its edges of iron
Were not fated to be enough to help
The man in battle—his hand was too strong.
That man, I heard, with his swing overtaxed
Every wound-hard weapon he had carried
Into battle—not any better for it.

Then for a third time was that stealthy brute,
That fire-fierce dragon, reminded of old feuds.
He rushed that hero when he got a chance,
Aggressively grim, went hot for the neck
With his bitter teeth. Beowulf throbbed red.
The life-blood of his soul rippled in gore.

Then I heard at his great prince's need
That Wiglaf showed such arm-work,
Such craft and keenness, as he was born to.
He never heeded the head, but burned his hand
Where he helped out with his family strength,
Striking this spiteful ghost with such spite
Low down, clever in arms, that his pretty sword
Plunged through plated flesh, and fire began
At last to cool. Beowulf was master still
Of arm and will and bared the bitter sharp
Dagger he bore on his smoldering byrnie.
The Weders' chief wrote the worm off across

The middle, felled his foe. Strong arms let life
Leak out—they had served him up together,
Two kinsmen pledged as man and knife should be,
Thanes at need! But that was the sinking king's
Last moment of winning work in this world.

From *Beowulf, An Edition and Literary Translation, In Progress*, edited and translated by Raymond P. Tripp, Jr., Denver, Colo.: The Society for New Language Study, 1990. Reprinted with minor editorial changes by permission of the translator.

The Dragon

Bartholomew Anglicus

While the medieval bestiaries treated animals as symbols of virtues and vices—portraying the dragon as an embodiment of evil—encyclopedias of the time tried to be more informative. Here is dragon lore from Mediaeval Lore from Bartholomew Anglicus, *the popular encyclopedia of Bartholomew Anglicus, "Bartholomew the Englishman," who died in 1264. St. Jerome was a biblical scholar.*

 he dragon is the largest of all serpents. Often he is drawn out of his den and rises up into the air, and the air is moved by him and also the sea swells against his venom. Often four or five of them fasten their tails together and rear up their heads and sail over seas and over rivers to get good meat. He has a crest with a little mouth and draws breath at small pipes and straight. He rears his tongue and has teeth like a saw. He has strength not only in teeth but also in tail and grieves both with biting and with stinging. He does not have as much venom as other serpents, but to slay his venom is not needed, for whom he binds he slays.

Jerome says that the dragon is a very thirsty beast. He opens his mouth against the wind to quench the burning of this thirst. Therefore, when he sees ships sail in the sea in great wind he flies against the sail to take their cold wind, and overthrows the ship sometimes by his size

---

of body and by a strong rush against the sail. When the shipmen see the dragon come near and know his coming by the water that swells against him, then they strike sail and escape in that way.

Between elephants and dragons is everlasting fighting, for the dragon with his tail binds and spans the elephant. The elephant with his foot and with his nose throws down the dragon. The dragon with his tail binds and spans the elephant's legs and makes him fall, but for that the dragon buys it full sore, for while he slays the elephant the elephant falls upon him and slays him.

From *Mediaeval Lore from Bartholomew Anglicus*, edited by Robert Steele. London: E. Stock, 1893. Reprint, New York: Cooper Square, 1966, pp.149-50.

Winged dragon. (Edward Topsell.)

The Dragon

The Winged Dragon

Edward Topsell

Ancient dragon lore, as well as lore of the unicorn, is collected in Edward Topsell's Historie of Foure-Footed Beasts *(1658). The woodcut from the book (see p. 118) portrays the airborne beast. "Voluble" means ease and rapidity of movement.*

here be some dragons which have wings and no feet, some again have both feet and wings, and some neither feet nor wings, but are only distinguished from the common sort of Serpents by the comb growing upon their heads, and the beard under their cheeks.

Saint Augustine saith that dragons do abide in deep Caves and hollow places of the earth, and that sometimes when they perceive moistness in the air, they come out of their holes, and beating the air with their wings, as it were with the strokes of Oars, they forsake the earth and fly aloft: which wings of theirs are of a skinny substance, and very voluble, and spreading themselves wide, according to the quantity and largeness of the Dragon's body, which caused Lucan the Poet in his verses to write in this manner following:

> You shining Dragons creeping on the earth,
> Which fiery Affrick holds with skins like gold,
> Yet pestilent by hot infecting breath:
> Mounted with wings in th' air we do behold.

The inhabitants of the kingdom of Georgia, once called Media, do say that in their Valleys there are divers Dragons which have both wings and feet, and that their feet are like unto the feet of Geese. Besides, there are dragons of sundry colours, for some of them are black, some red, some of an ash-colour, some yellow, and their shape and outward appearance very beautiful. . . .

Gyllius, Pierius, and Gervinus . . . do affirm that a Dragon is of a black colour, the belly somewhat green, and very beautiful to behold, having a treble row of teeth in their mouths upon every jaw, and with most bright and clear-seeing eyes, which caused the Poets to say in their writings that these dragons are the watchful keepers of Treasures. They have also two dewlaps growing under their chin, and hanging down like a beard, which are of a red colour: their bodies are set all over with very sharp scales, and over their eyes stand certain flexible eyelids. When they gape wide with their mouth, and thrust forth their tongue, their teeth seem very much to resemble the teeth of wild Swine: And their necks have many times gross thick hair growing upon them, much like unto the bristles of a wild Boar.

Their mouth, (especially of the most tamable Dragons) is but little, not much bigger than a pipe, through which they draw in their breath, for they wound not with their mouth, but with their tails, only beating with them when they are angry. But the Indian, Ethiopian, and Phrygian dragons have very wide mouths, through which they often swallow in whole fowls and beasts. Their tongue is cloven as it were double, and the Investigators of nature do say that they have fifteen teeth of a side. The males have combs on their heads, but the females have none, and they are likewise distinguished by their beards.

From *The Historie of Foure-Footed Beasts* by Edward Topsell. London, 1658; Ann Arbor, Mich.: University Microfilms, 1962.

The Dragon Around the World

The dragon is the most universal of fabulous beasts. A gigantic serpentine being with supernatural powers, it has appeared in different forms from Egypt to China to the Americas. From myth to folklore, the dragon spread from one culture to another and emerged in different societies, with local haunts and individual personalities. Nearly every group of people seems to have needed a dragon-like creature of its own.

The Oriental Dragon

While monstrous Western dragons were being slain by gods and heroes to attain treasure or rescue fair maidens, the dragon of the East multiplied into a host of benevolent emperors of earth, sea, and sky. The spirit of change and of life itself, the Eastern dragons make themselves visible or invisible at will and are able to shift their form and size.

The most common image of the Chinese dragon is all energy: a whirling, twisting form, flickering like flames, leaping and laughing among the clouds. From its maned, horse-like head grow horns that serve it as ears. Long whiskers curl from its bearded muzzle. A ridge of eighty-one points grows down its scaly back. Sometimes it has wings. If it is an Imperial Dragon, five

Chinese imperial dragon.

claws curve from its feet. If it is a local dragon, it has four claws. Able to change its size, the dragon can expand itself to fill the sky or reduce itself to the size of a worm—or even disappear altogether, and appear again.

Paintings and embroideries often show the dragon reaching out for, or playing with, a ball of light. This sacred pearl is usually bluish white, gold, or red. It has been interpreted as a symbol of rolling thunder, the sun, the moon, a cosmic egg, and the pearl of truth. Some say it contains the dragon's power and that if it is stolen, the dragon loses its strength.

Traditionally, the most powerful dragon is the Lung, which rules the sky. It is said to be made up of nine different animals: a camel's head, a deer's horns, a devil's eyes, an ox's ears, a snake's neck, a clam's belly, a fish's scales, an eagle's talons, and a tiger's paws. Its breath forms clouds, and its voice is like "the jingling of copper pans." Its favorite food is roasted swallows.

The dragons are weather lords, ruling water, rain, clouds, the thunder, and lightning. They rise from the sea in waterspouts and typhoons. They form clouds, and when dragons fight in the sky, they raise the wind, flash lightning, and roar with thunder. The *Li* is the chief dragon of the ocean, and the *Chiao* the dragon of earth.

Others are the Celestial Dragon, the Spiritual Dragon, the Dragon of Hidden Treasures, the Winged Dragon, the Horned Dragon, the Coiling Dragon, and the Yellow Dragon. Four dragon kings rule the four oceans from their jeweled, undersea palaces. And each of nine individual species is associated with a particular object, such as a bell, a monument, a temple, a bridge, and a sword hilt. It is said that somewhere in the sky is a tablet containing the number of dragons in the universe.

Chinese dragon.

The five-toed Imperial Dragon is the emblem of Chinese emperors, embroidered on robes and on banners, and the emperors were themselves traced back to dragons. The first emperor was said to have a dragon's tail. One rode a dragon to the heavens. Dragons pulled the chariots of emperors through sky and sea.

Processional dragons made of sticks, paper, and cloth still herald the New Year, and boats with dragon-head prows and dragon-tail sterns race against each other in annual Dragon Boat Festivals.

Tetsu

In Japan, the dragon is called Tetsu and has three claws.

The Nagas

The dragon-like naga of India has the head and torso of a human and the body of a snake. Like the dragons of China, different groups of nagas cause clouds and rain, guard treasure, protect palaces and temples, dwell in springs and rivers, and live in palaces under the sea. They, too, have a divine pearl.

Quetzalcoatl

The plumed serpent of ancient Mexico was a combination of the rare quetzal bird and a serpent. He was a god of wind and water, bringing rain and fertility to the desert, and arcing himself across the sky as a shimmering rainbow. He created human beings, taught them the arts, and revealed to them the mineral treasures of the earth. After Quetzalcoatl quarreled with other gods, he left the land on a raft of snakes, followed by flocks of brilliantly feathered birds. He vowed to return in the year 1519.

Historically, Cortez and the Spanish conquistadors arrived in Mexico in 1519. The Aztec king, Montezuma, believing Cortez to be Quetzalcoatl, granted the Spaniard all the treasure and power he desired. Thus weakened by their belief, the Aztecs were conquered by the Spanish.

Quetzalcoatl.

Piasa

While exploring the Mississippi River in 1675, the French priest Jacques Marquette came upon paintings of two monsters on a rocky cliff overlooking rough water. These petroglyphs depicted human-headed creatures with deer antlers, scaly bodies, and long tails that wound over the beast and back between its legs. Sketches of the Piasa [PIE-ah-saw] include fangs, eagle talons, and spiny wings. Father Marquette's Native American guides showed great respect for the painted monster, whose name means "the bird that devours men."

In Alton, Illinois, the site of the paintings, the Piasa is a tourist attraction. A new metal sign picturing the monster is attached to a cliff near the town, and the Piasa glowers from tee-shirts and postcards. The town's mascot, the story goes, carried off deer and people for dinner until one brave warrior shot it with poison arrows.

Like Chinese dragons and the nagas of India, the Piasa and other monsters of Native American lore were associated with water. These creatures lived in springs, rivers, and lakes. They caused storms, overturned boats, and drowned swimmers. Tribes from the Mississippi Valley and Great Lakes commonly drew monsters on cliffs above dangerous rapids and whirlpools.

Mo-o

Mo-o [Mo-ko] is the dragon of the Polynesians. Its name is the Polynesian word for great sea creatures. Around 1850, when oysters were becoming scarce, natives thought a Mo-o that lived in what is now Pearl Harbor moved the oysters to a distant land.

Sea Serpents

One form of water monster is the sea serpent, a dragon-like creature with a bearded or crested horse-like head and a long, serpentine body. People from California to Sweden have reported seeing such beasts in freshwater lakes, and nineteenth-century sea captains commonly sighted sea serpents in the North Atlantic Ocean. The most famous of these creatures is "Nessie," the Loch Ness Monster, whose existence is still a matter of emotional debate. One scientific finding surmises that Nessie is a large sturgeon.

The Universal Dragon

Like the Cosmic Serpent of old, dragon lore encircles the world. In local legend, in folk and fairy tales, and in mythology, the dragon appears in different shapes—as fire-breathing worm and drake, jungle serpent, powers of the skies and seas, feathered serpent, and monster of the waters. By virtue of the sheer number and forms of dragon tales from country to country, the dragon is definitely the king of wonder beasts.

Sea serpent from *Olaus Magnus*.

The Student and the Dragon King

Chinese Fairy Tale

The dragons of China are water lords, controlling clouds and rain, rivers and seas. They live in splendor in underwater palaces, and they can change their shape and size at will. This story, retold by Joe Nigg, is based upon a traditional tale.

ong ago, a student named Liu was walking home along the banks of the River Ching. Spring was in the blossoming plum trees and in the warm air, but he was sad because he had just failed his university examinations.

He came upon a young woman herding goats along the path. Although she was doing peasant work and was wearing a dirty, tattered dress, she moved with regal grace. Her face was beautiful, but she, too, was sad. Liu bowed to the strange goatherd and asked if he could be of service to her.

She looked at him with sad, jade-green eyes and asked if he truly meant what he said.

Now a little uncertain, Liu thought for a moment and said yes, he would be pleased to help her in any way he could.

"Then I would like you to take this letter to my father," she said, pulling a rolled paper from her sleeve.

"It's already written," he said, surprised.

"I have been waiting for someone willing to help me," she said.

Hesitating, Liu took the letter, which was sealed with what looked like a royal crest. "Where does your father live?" he asked.

"Not far," she said. "Go to the north shore of Tung Ting Lake and strike the tallest tree three times with your belt."

Liu was puzzled, but he said he would do as she asked.

As the strange goatherd thanked him, her damp eyes shone.

While walking to the lake, Liu marveled at the strangeness of the day. He sighted the tallest tree on the north shore of Lake Tung Ting and made his way towards it.

When he reached the tree, he took off his belt and hit it against the trunk three times. As he stood there in the silence, looking at the shining water, he wondered who the girl's father was and where he lived.

The water glinted silver with sunlight. Sparks of gold and crimson flashed beneath the surface. The water stirred, and the back of a great red carp glided straight towards him. As it reached the shore, a boy in green silk rose from the water at his feet.

"Are you the one who struck the tree three times?" the boy asked.

Liu nodded.

"You are in the power of dragons," the boy said and instructed Liu to climb upon his back.

The student could now do only as he was told, but that did not keep him from feeling fear when the boy carried him into the lake. As the water rose over them, the green boy changed into a red carp.

Liu was amazed that he was not drowning but was riding a great red fish down through liquid light.

Ahead of them appeared a shimmering undersea palace. As they glided nearer, it grew in size and splendor. Its walls glowed with colorful coral and shone with pearls. Laughing jade dragons twisted and curled from the tower roofs.

The carp beneath him became the boy in green silk, standing in front of him, his clothes completely dry. The green boy led him through opening doors into a vast golden hall, its vaulted ceiling so high it was lost in light. Rows of figures in robes of green and silver scales stretched to the end of the immense room. At the far end, on a raised throne carved with dragons, sat a bearded man in an embroidered dragon robe.

The green boy led Liu between the rows of courtiers, up to the throne itself. The man rose, towering over them, taller than mortal.

"I am the Dragon King," he said. "Welcome to my palace."

Liu bowed deeply.

"How did you know the secret of the tree?" the Dragon King asked.

"Your honorable daughter asked me to bring you a letter." Liu said. "She told me to go to the tallest tree on the north shore of Tung Ting Lake and strike it with my belt three times."

Liu pulled the letter from his sleeve, noticed the paper was dry, and handed it to the green boy, who carried it up to the Dragon King.

The Dragon King broke the seal, unrolled the letter, and read it standing. His features clouded with rage.

Liu stepped back. Down the throne room, the courtiers leaned forward.

The Dragon King composed himself and spoke with great sadness: "The Princess has been basely and cruelly treated by her River Dragon

The Dragon

husband. He has cast her from his palace and forced her to work like a slave."

The courtiers shivered with horror and began to weep.

"Someone fetch the Queen," the Dragon King said. "She, also, must learn of this insult to our family."

The Queen was summoned, and when she heard the news, she, too, began to weep.

As the weeping turned to wailing and the hall reverberated with grief, Liu looked around in fear, not knowing what might happen next.

The Dragon King held up his hands to quiet the court. "Silence," he said. "We cannot let Chien Tang know the fate of the Princess. If he ever learns of her treatment at the hands of the River Dragon, no chain will hold him."

Liu looked at the green boy, who stepped closer to him and whispered that Chien Tang was the brother of the Dragon King. The Princess had been his favorite, and when her father gave her in marriage to the River Dragon, Chien Tang thrashed his tail with such anger that he created a tidal wave that washed away whole villages. For this, the Supreme Dragon sentenced him to be chained to a pillar beneath the palace for all eternity.

Liu turned toward the great doors at the end of the hall. The floor began to tremble beneath his feet, and the walls of the palace groaned. A thunderous clamor rose from below, and through the doors, wide-clawed and breathing fire, Chien Tang stormed into the hall, a thousand feet of swirling red body, dragging the chained pillar behind him.

Everyone fell to the floor as the enraged dragon whirled through the hall like a typhoon, the pillar smashing into walls, shaking the palace to its foundations.

Then he was gone.

In the silence, Liu looked up from the floor. Around the hall, the courtiers stirred, and sat up. They were all standing and looking about when Chien Tang flew back into the room.

The courtiers screamed and recoiled in horror at first. Then, they saw the Princess riding on the dragon's back, and they shouted for joy.

Chien Tang landed, his head at the foot of the throne. His red scaly body uncurled the length of the hall. The Princess slipped from his back and into the open arms of the Dragon King and Queen.

Liu reached out to touch the dragon, but even as he stretched out his arm, Chien Tang shrank from a thousand feet, to hundreds, to six, and stood, a man closely resembling his Dragon King brother.

"The River Dragon is no longer," Chien Tang said. "The pillar dropped off when the Supreme Dragon pardoned me. And your daughter is home at last."

"And it's all because of him," the Princess said, looking at Liu with bright, jade-green eyes.

Liu glanced at the green boy. "No, no," he said. "Not really."

"Yes, really," the Dragon King said. "Even though you are a mere mortal, your courage has brought us all together again. For that, I offer you a dragon's life of ten thousand years, in water as well as air. And," he said, looking at the Princess, "that is, if our daughter agrees . . ."

The Princess beamed and nodded.

"No, I couldn't," Liu said. He shook his head and shifted his weight from one foot to the other. "I'm unworthy. I couldn't even pass my examinations."

The Dragon King laughed. "You don't mean you're not smart enough to become my son-in-law."

Liu smiled, elated. "That's right. I don't mean that," he said humbly.

"It is time for celebration!" said the Dragon King.

Rejoicing filled the great hall.

Tables were set from one end of the thousand-foot room to the other, and for hours on end the court was served a sumptuous dragon feast such as none of them had ever before known.

Retold by Joe Nigg.

The Lambton Worm

English Folktale

In the tradition of Beowulf, Siegfried, and St. George, knights battle dragons in innumerable stories. Sometimes the hero's armor is fashioned to the task. In this tale, retold by Joe Nigg, the Heir of Lambton dons special steel to fight the dreaded Worm. The Heir's armor is similar to that of another knight, More of More Hall, who fought the Dragon of Wantley.

 here are hills in England whose ridges, people say, were formed by dragons coiled upon the earth. Worm Hill, in the county of Durham, is one of these. The beast that lived upon the hill changed the history of the ancient Lambton family, who lived in a manor on the banks of the river Wear.

Long ago, there was a particularly wild and careless young Heir of Lambton. On Sunday mornings, others on their way to church would see him fishing and hear him swearing at his bad luck. One Sunday, after the servants and tenants passed him, shaking their heads, the Heir's pole bent with a heavy catch. He excitedly reeled in his prize only to recoil in disgust at an ugly, writhing lizard-like creature with nine holes around its mouth. The Heir yanked out the hook and flung the loathsome thing into a well, known to this day as Worm Well.

Just then a stranger passing by asked him if he had had any luck. "Bad luck," the Heir answered. "My catch looks like the Devil himself." The stranger peered down into the well, grimaced, and agreed that the ugly thing could mean no good.

When he grew older, the Heir renounced his early, wicked ways and went off to join the Crusades. All this time, the Worm in the well had continued to grow. One night it crawled out of its confined place and coiled itself around a rock in the middle of the Wear. Then it slithered up onto a nearby hill, about a mile and a half across the river from Lambton Hall. The beast continued to grow, until its length coiled around the mound three times. Its weight shaped the earth into ridges that can still be seen on Worm Hill near the river Wear.

The Worm began to terrorize the countryside, sucking the cows dry, devouring the lambs, and driving people out of their homes. The north side of the Wear was a wasted land by the time the monster crossed the stream and headed for Lambton Hall, where the aging lord of the manor lived alone with his servants. People fleeing from across the river warned the Lambton household of the approach of the terrible Worm.

The only thing to be done, said the old steward, was to fill the large trough in the courtyard with milk to satisfy the hunger of the beast. This the servants did without delay, filling the trough to the brim with the milk of nine cows. Then everyone gathered in the manor and watched with wide-eyed fear as the Worm dragged its great length up to the hall. The ugly beast with nine holes around its mouth swung its head from side to side as it surveyed the grounds, saw the trough, and lapped it dry. Milk streaming from its jaws, it turned and lurched off toward the river. The people watched it cross the swift water and move off to its hill, where it wrapped itself around the slope and slept.

The next morning, when the Worm roused itself and again crossed the Wear, the steward again had the servants fill the trough with milk. As before, the Worm approached the manor, saw the milk, emptied the trough, and returned to its hill. The same thing happened day after day. The few times the trough was not filled to the brim, the monster roared, and lashing its tail in rage, pulled trees out of the ground and flung them into the air.

Hearing of the Worm's devastation, knights from around the North Country came to battle the beast. One by one, they learned at the cost of life or limb that in addition to its size and strength, the Worm had the awful power to reunite itself after it had been severed into pieces.

After an absence of seven long years, the Heir returned to find his ancestral lands laid waste, the people oppressed, and his father dying sick of heart. He soon came to realize that the cause of all this grief was no other than the loathsome thing he himself had pulled from the river Wear and flung into the well. Filled with remorse, the Heir vowed to make amends for what he had done so long before.

The first thing he did was consult the Wise Woman of Lambton, a sibyl who lived at the edge of Lambton Wood. She immediately condemned him for bringing destruction upon his family and the entire region. But after she saw how penitent he was and how determined to right the wrong, she agreed to offer him her wisdom. What he needed to do, she said, was stud his armor with the sharp points of spears and meet the monster on the rocks in the middle of the foaming Wear. She added, though, that he must vow that if he defeated the beast, he must kill the first living thing he met on his way home from the river. If he failed to fulfill that vow, she said, nine generations of the house of Lambton would not die in their beds. In exchange for her wisdom, the Heir reluctantly made the vow.

So he took his armor to the family smith and told him to stud it with spear points. He told the household about the vow the Wise Woman demanded of him. The old steward proposed that upon hearing a single blast of the victorious Heir's hunting horn, he would release the family hound to greet its master. The Heir sadly agreed with the choice of sacrifice.

When his new armor was complete, the Heir donned the pointed steel and strapped on his sword. The servants sat locked within the hall as he waded out to the rocks in the river and waited for the Worm to cross on its daily foray to Lambton Hall.

The sun was high when the Heir saw Worm Hill move with scales, and with wildly beating heart and weak legs, he watched the beast lumber down to the water. Catching sight of the armored Heir upon the rocks, the creature stopped, bellowed, and plunged into the swirling stream, heading straight towards him. The Heir braced himself, and as the Worm lunged up out of the water, he swung the sword with all his might. The Worm howled and coiled itself around the knight. It writhed in pain as the spikes pierced its scales. Its blood streamed into the water. The Heir hacked at the coils round his legs. A twisting piece of the monster dropped into the stream and floated away. Then another piece. And another. All the pieces were carried away by the current. Unable to reunite itself, its lifeblood flowing over the rock, the Worm at last relaxed its hold upon the knight and tumbled into the river Wear. The Heir collapsed with exhaustion upon the rock.

It was dusk when the servants of Lambton Hall heard the welcome blast of the hunting horn. In his rooms, the aging Lord also heard the call. Knowing his son had set out to meet the Worm and fearing for the young man's safety, he forgot the plan agreed upon and rushed out of the manor to embrace the Heir. The Heir was horrified to see his father hurrying towards him. He could not kill his father to fulfill the vow. In desperation he blew the horn again. By this time the old steward had released the dog, which raced across the grounds towards its master. The anguished Heir raised the sword still red with the monster's blood and killed the family hound.

But the Heir's action was in vain. In spite of his bravery that day, the broken vow brought down the sibyl's curse upon the House of Lambton, and for nine generations no one of that house died in his bed.

Why the Moon and the Stars Receive Their Light from the Sun

Ashanti Folktale

The sharp-sighted, fire-breathing dragon in this spirited Ashanti tale from Ghana is anything but conventional as it pursues its prey from earth to sky. Anansi the Spider is the celebrated trickster-hero of West African folklore. This story is from West African Folk-Tales, *collected by W. H. Barker and Cecilia Sinclair.*

nce upon a time there was a great scarcity of food in the land. Father Anansi and his son, Kweku Tsin, being very hungry, set out one morning to hunt in the forest. In a short time Kweku Tsin was fortunate enough to kill a fine deer— which he carried to his father at their resting-place. Anansi was very glad to see such a supply of food, and requested his son to remain there on guard, while he went for a large basket in which to carry it home. An hour or so passed without his return, and Kweku Tsin became anxious. Fearing lest his father had lost his way, he called out loudly, "Father, Father!" to guide him to the spot. To his joy he heard a voice reply, "Yes, my son," and immediately he shouted again, thinking it was Anansi. Instead of the latter, however, a terrible dragon appeared. This monster breathed fire from his great nostrils, and was altogether a dreadful sight to behold. Kweku Tsin was terrified at his approach and speedily hid himself in a cave near by.

The dragon arrived at the resting-place, and was much annoyed to find only the deer's body. He vented his anger in blows upon the latter and went away. Soon after, Father Anansi made his appearance. He was greatly interested in his son's tale, and wished to see the dragon for himself. He soon had his desire, for the monster, smelling human flesh, hastily returned to the spot and seized them both. They were carried off by him to his castle, where they found many other unfortunate creatures also awaiting their fate. All were left in charge of the dragon's servant—a fine, white cock—which always crowed to summon his master, if anything unusual happened in the latter's absence. The dragon then went off in search of more prey.

Kweku Tsin now summoned all his fellow-prisoners together, to arrange a way of escape. All feared to run away—because of the wonderful powers of the monster. His eyesight was so keen that he could detect a fly moving miles away. Not only that, but he could move over the ground so swiftly that none could outdistance him. Kweku Tsin, however, being exceedingly clever, soon thought of a plan.

Knowing that the white cock would not crow as long as he had grains of rice to pick up, Kweku scattered on the ground the contents of forty bags of grain—which were stored in the great hall. While the cock was thus busily engaged, Kweku Tsin ordered the spinners to spin fine hempen ropes, to make a strong rope ladder. One end of this he intended to throw up to heaven, trusting that the gods would catch it and hold it fast, while he and his fellow-prisoners mounted.

While the ladder was being made, the men killed and ate all the cattle they needed—reserving all the bones for Kweku Tsin at his express desire. When all was ready the young man gathered the bones into a great sack. He also procured the dragon's fiddle and placed it by his side.

Everything was now ready. Kweku Tsin threw one end of the ladder up to the sky. It was caught and held. The dragon's victims began to mount, one after the other, Kweku remaining at the bottom.

By this time, however, the monster's powerful eyesight showed him that something unusual was happening at his abode. He hastened his return. On seeing his approach, Kweku Tsin also mounted the ladder—with the bag of bones on his back, and the fiddle under his arm. The dragon began to climb after him. Each time the monster came too near the young man threw him a bone, with which, being very hungry, he was obliged to descend to the ground to eat.

Kweku Tsin repeated this performance till all the bones were gone, by which time the people were safely up in the heavens. Then he mounted himself, as rapidly as possible, stopping every now and then to play a tune on the wonderful fiddle. Each time he did this, the dragon had to return to earth, to dance—as he could not resist the magic music. When Kweku was quite close to the top, the dragon had very nearly reached him again. The brave youth bent down and cut the ladder away below his own feet. The dragon was dashed to the ground—but Kweku was pulled up into safety by the gods.

The latter were so pleased with his wisdom and bravery in giving freedom to his fellow-men, that they made him the sun—the source of all light and heat to the world. His father, Anansi, became the moon, and his friends the stars. Thereafter, it was Kweku Tsin's privilege to supply all these with light, each being dull and powerless without him.

From *West African Folk-Tales* by W. H. Barker and Cecilia Sinclair. London: George G. Harrap, 1917, pp. 97-101.

The Dragon Today

We now believe that the dragon of the imagination grew from actual crocodiles, giant constrictors, lizards, and the fossilized bones of saurian creatures.

An animal described as a horrible twenty-foot monster living in the jungles of Komodo Island, in Indonesia, was for a time thought to be legendary, but there were so many eyewitness reports of the beast that a small 1912 expedition was organized to find it. The Komodo dragon turned out to be a ten-foot-long lizard, the largest lizard on earth. During later highly publicized expeditions in the 1920s, many of the Komodo dragons were either shot or were captured and sent back to European zoos. Dragon-like sea serpents were commonly sighted in the nineteenth century, and many people still watch for what is now the most famous of the breed, Nessie, the Loch Ness Monster.

The Western dragon of the imagination, meanwhile, continued to develop and change. Children's literature often turned the terrible nightmare monster into a large and lovable pet. Fantasy and science fiction, both in books and on film, transported the dragon to distant worlds. It became a star of fantasy games.

Still, the traditional dragon is very much with us, in museum paintings and sculpture, in heraldry and national emblems. Its Asian counterpart lives in Far Eastern art, architecture, furniture, on tea boxes, and in Oriental restaurants around the world. And this very night the constellation Draco will twist through northern skies.

Tale of the Computer That Fought a Dragon

Stanislaw Lem

As long as there have been Western dragons, there have been dragon slayers, from the Babylonian Marduk, to Saint George, to the latest fantasy hero. In this playful science fiction tale, the ruler of a robotic kingdom enlists the most modern of champions to rid his kingdom of a fearsome beast. Throughout the story, the author creates puns out of "cyber," from "cybernetics," relating to robots.

ing Poleander Partobon, ruler of Cyberia, was a great warrior, and being an advocate of the methods of modern strategy, above all else he prized cybernetics as a military art. His kingdom swarmed with thinking machines, for Poleander put them everywhere he could; not merely in the astronomical observatories or the schools, but he ordered electric brains mounted in the rocks upon the roads, which with loud voices cautioned pedestrians against tripping; also in posts, in walls, in trees, so that one could ask directions anywhere when lost; he stuck them onto clouds, so they could announce the rain in advance, he added them to the hills and valleys—in short, it was impossible to walk on Cyberia without bumping into an intelligent machine. The planet was beautiful, since the King not only gave decrees for the cybernetic perfecting of that which had long been in existence, but he introduced by law entirely new orders of things. Thus for example in his kingdom were manufactured cyberbeetles and buzzing cyberbees, and even cyberflies—these would be seized by mechanical spiders when they grew too numerous. On the planet cyberbosks of cybergorse rustled in the wind, cybercalliopes and cyberviols sang—but besides these civilian devices, there were twice as many military, for the King was most bellicose. In his palace vaults he had a strategic computer, a machine of uncommon mettle; he had smaller ones also, and divisions of cybersaries, enormous cybermatics and a whole arsenal of every other kind of weapon, including powder. There was only this one problem, and it troubled him greatly, namely, that he had not a single adversary or enemy and no one in any way wished to invade his land, and thereby provide him with the opportunity to demonstrate his kingly and terrifying courage, his tactical genius, not to mention the simply extraordinary effectiveness of his cybernetic weaponry. In the absence of genuine enemies and aggressors the King had his engineers build artificial ones, and against these he did battle, and always won. However inasmuch as the battles and campaigns were genuinely dreadful, the populace suffered no little injury from them. The subjects murmured when all too many cyberfoes had destroyed their settlements and towns, when the synthetic enemy poured liquid fire upon them; they even dared voice their discontent when the King himself, issuing forth as their deliverer and vanquishing the artificial foe, in the course of the victorious attacks laid waste to everything that stood in his path. They grumbled even then, the ingrates, though the thing was done on their behalf.

Until the King wearied of the war games on the planet and decided to raise his sights. Now it was cosmic wars and sallies that he dreamed of. His planet had a large Moon, entirely desolate and wild; the King laid heavy taxes upon his subjects, to obtain the funds needed to build whole armies on that Moon and have there a new theater of war. And the subjects were more than happy to pay, figuring that King Poleander would now no longer deliver them with his cybermatics, nor test the strength of his arms upon their homes and heads. And so the royal engineers built on the Moon a splendid computer, which in turn was to create all manner of troops and self-firing gunnery. The King lost no time in testing the machine's prowess this way and that; at one point he ordered it—by telegraph—to execute a volt-vault electrosault: for he wanted to see if it was true, what his engineers had told him, that the machine could do anything. If it can do anything, he thought, then let it do a flip. However the text of the telegram underwent a slight distortion and the machine received the order that it was to execute not an electrosault, but an electrosaur—and this it carried out as best it could.

Meanwhile the King conducted one more campaign, liberating some provinces of his realm seized by cyberknechts; he completely forgot about the order given the computer on the Moon, then suddenly giant boulders came hurtling down from there; the King was astounded, for one even fell on the wing of the palace and destroyed his prize collection of cyberads, which are dryads with feedback. Fuming he telegraphed the Moon computer at once, demanding an explanation. It didn't reply however, for it no longer was: the electrosaur had swallowed it and made it into its own tail.

Immediately the King dispatched an entire armed expedition to the Moon, placing at its head another computer, also very valiant, to slay the dragon, but there was only some flashing, some rumbling, and then no more computer nor expedition; for the electrodragon wasn't pretend and wasn't pretending, but battled with the utmost verisimili-tude, and had moreover the worst of intentions regarding the kingdom and the King. The King sent to the Moon his cybernants, cyberneers, cyberines, and lieutenant cybernets, at the very end he even sent one cyberalissimo, but it too accomplished nothing; the hurly-burly lasted a little longer, that was all. The King watched through a telescope set up on the palace balcony.

The dragon grew, the Moon became smaller and smaller since the monster was devouring it piecemeal and incorporating it into its own body. The King saw then, and his subjects did also, that things were serious, for when the ground beneath the feet of the electrosaur was gone, it would for certain hurl itself upon the planet and upon them. The King thought and thought, but he saw no remedy, and knew not what to do. To send machines was no good, for they would be lost, and to go himself was no better, for he was afraid. Suddenly the King heard, in the stillness of the night, the telegraph chattering from his royal bedchamber. It was the King's personal receiver, solid gold with a diamond needle, linked to the Moon; the King jumped up and ran to it, the apparatus meanwhile went tap-tap, tap-tap, and tapped out this telegram: THE DRAGON SAYS POLEANDER PARTOBON BETTER CLEAR OUT BECAUSE HE THE DRAGON INTENDS TO OCCUPY THE THRONE!

The King took fright, quaked from head to toe, and ran, just as he was, in his ermine nightshirt and slippers, down to the palace vaults, where stood the strategy machine, old and very wise. He had not as yet consulted it, since prior to the rise and uprise of the electrodragon they had argued on the subject of a certain military operation; but now was not the time to think of that—his throne, his life was at stake!

He plugged it in, and as soon as it warmed up he cried:

"My old computer! My good computer! It's this way and that, the dragon wishes to deprive me of my throne, to cast me out, help, speak, how can I defeat it?!"

"Uh-uh," said the computer. "First you must admit I was right in that previous business, and secondly, I would have you address me only as Digital Grand Vizier, though you may also say to me: 'Your Ferromagneticity'!"

"Good, good, I'll name you Grand Vizier, I'll agree to anything you like, only save me!"

The machine whirred, chirred, hummed, hemmed, then said:

"It is a simple matter. We build an electrosaur more powerful than the one located on the Moon. It will defeat the lunar one, settle its circuitry once and for all and thereby attain the goal!"

"Perfect!" replied the King. "And can you make a blueprint of this dragon?"

"It will be an ultradragon," said the computer. "And I can make you not only a blueprint, but the thing itself, which I shall now do, it won't take a minute, King!" And true to its word, it hissed, it chugged, it whistled and buzzed, assembling something down within itself, and already an object like a giant claw, sparking, arcing, was emerging from its side, when the King shouted:

"Old computer! Stop!"

"Is this how you address me? I am the Digital Grand Vizier!"

"Ah, of course," said the King. "Your Ferromagneticity, the electrodragon you are making will defeat the other dragon, granted, but it will surely remain in the other's place, how then are we to get rid of it in turn?!"

"Ah, now that's a different matter," the computer replied. "Why didn't you say so in the first place? You see how illogically you express yourself? One moment . . . I must think."

And it churred and hummed, and chuffed and chuckled, and finally said:

"We make an antimoon with an antidragon, place it in the Moon's orbit (here something went snap inside), sit around the fire and sing: *Oh I'm a robot full of fun, water doesn't scare me none, I dives right in, I gives a grin, tra la the livelong day!!*"

"You speak strangely," said the King. "What does the antimoon have to do with that song about the funny robot?"

"What funny robot?" asked the computer. "Ah, no, no, I made a mistake, something feels wrong inside, I must have blown a tube." The King began to look for the trouble, finally found the burnt-out tube, put in a new one, then asked the computer about the antimoon.

"What antimoon?" asked the computer, which meanwhile had forgotten what it said before. "I don't know anything about an antimoon . . . one moment, I have to give this thought."

It hummed, it huffed, and it said:

"We create a general theory of the slaying of electrodragons, of which the lunar dragon will be a special case, its solution trivial."

"Well, create such a theory!" said the King.

"To do this I must first create various experimental dragons."

"Certainly not! No thank you!" exclaimed the King. "A dragon wants to deprive me of my throne, just think what might happen if you produced a swarm of them!"

"Oh? Well then, in that case we must resort to other means. We will use a strategic variant of the method of successive approximations. Go and telegraph the dragon that you will give it the throne on the condition that it perform three mathematical operations, really quite simple . . ."

The King went and telegraphed, and the dragon agreed. The King returned to the computer.

"Now," it said, "here is the first operation: tell it to divide itself by itself!"

The King did this. The electrosaur divided itself by itself, but since one electrosaur over one electrosaur is one, it remained on the Moon and nothing changed.

"Is this the best you can do?!" cried the King, running into the vault with such haste, that his slippers fell off. "The dragon divided itself by itself, but since one goes into one once, nothing changed!"

"That's all right, I did that on purpose, the operation was to divert attention," said the computer. "And now tell it to extract its root!" The King telegraphed to the Moon, and the dragon began to pull, push, pull, push, until it crackled from the strain, panted, trembled all over, but suddenly something gave—and it extracted its own root!

The King went back to the computer.

"The dragon crackled, trembled, even ground its teeth, but extracted the root and threatens me still!" he shouted from the doorway. "What now, my old . . . I mean, Your Ferromagneticity?!"

"Be of stout heart," it said. "Now go tell it to subtract itself from itself!"

The King hurried to his royal bedchamber, sent the telegram and the dragon began to subtract itself from itself, taking away its tail first, then legs, then trunk, and finally, when it saw that something wasn't right, it hesitated, but from its own momentum the subtracting continued, it took away its head and became zero, in other words nothing: the electrosaur was no more!

"The electrosaur is no more," cried the joyful King, bursting into the vault. "Thank you, old computer . . . many thanks . . . you have worked hard . . . you have earned a rest, so now I will disconnect you."

"Not so fast, my dear," the computer replied. "I do the job and you want to disconnect me, and you no longer call me Your Ferromagneticity?! That's not nice, not nice at all! Now I myself will change into an electrosaur, yes, and drive you from the kingdom, and most certainly rule better than you, for you always consulted me in all the more important matters, therefore it was really I who ruled all along, and not you . . . "

And huffing, puffing, it began to change into an electrosaur; flaming electroclaws were already protruding from its sides when the King, breathless with fright, tore the slippers off his feet, rushed up to it and with the slippers began beating blindly at its tubes! The computer chugged, choked, and got muddled in its program—instead of the word "electrosaur" it read "electrosauce," and before the King's very eyes the computer, wheezing more and more softly, turned into an enormous, gleaming-golden heap of electrosauce, which, still sizzling, emitted all its charge in deep-blue sparks, leaving Poleander to stare dumbstruck at only a great, steaming pool of gravy . . .

With a sigh the King put on his slippers and returned to the royal bedchamber. However from that time on he was an altogether different king: the events he had undergone made his nature less bellicose, and to the end of his days he engaged exclusively in civilian cybernetics, and left the military kind strictly alone.

From *The Cosmic Carnival of Stanislaw Lem: An Anthology of Entertaining Stories by the Modern Master of Science Fiction*, edited by Michael Kandel. New York: Continuum, 1981, pp. 170-77.

More Wonder Beasts

More Wonder Beasts

esides the four major wonder beasts—the phoenix, griffin, unicorn, and dragon—and their close relatives, there are so many other mythical and fabulous creatures from around the world that it takes whole books to hold them all. Hundreds of pages separate the *A Boa A Qu* from the *Zu*. And that does not even take into account the host of newly invented creatures that throng through popular culture, from the Star Wars trilogy to board games and video games. There were probably several new fantastic beasts born today, and there will be more tomorrow. We can all create our own by combining the parts and powers of various animals in our own imaginations.

One way to and see how many kinds of fantastic creatures and wonder beasts in general have changed over the ages is to put an ancient passage beside a modern one, such as the two selections below.

We met the Roman writer Pliny the Elder earlier in this book when he described the phoenix of Egypt and the griffins of Scythia. Of the many volumes of his *Natural History*, one that has always been the most popular contained descriptions of marvels, including wonder beasts. Pliny treated most of the creatures as actual animals in faraway lands, and for many centuries afterwards, other scholars simply repeated what he had written.

By the time the griffin sings in Barbara Wersba's book for young readers, *The Land of Forgotten Beasts*, people no longer believed in it and the other wonder beasts. As long as people accepted what Pliny and other authorities had said, the wonder beasts were safe. But when the new science rejected the old books, the wonder beasts were rejected right along with them.

The phoenix and the rest were scorned as fabulous animals, worthless fantasy. And for a time, they withdrew to the Land of Forgotten Beasts—a fate that might lie ahead for our own modern monsters, the controversial "Nessie," Bigfoot, and the Abominable Snowman.

Many of Pliny's wonder beasts have indeed been forgotten, living on only in books of arcane lore. Some reappeared in different form in children's literature, and then in fantasy and science fiction.

Here, then, is a host of wonder beasts.

Wonder Beasts of Ethiopia

Pliny the Elder

The Roman naturalist and encyclopedist Pliny parades an entire menagerie of wonder beasts past us in his Natural History. *He matter-of-factly introduces each one as an actual animal from an exotic land. Along with some actual animals and assorted bizarre creatures, there are the yale, with the movable horns; the manticore, with triple rows of teeth; the sluggish but deadly catoblepas; and the basilisk (cockatrice), whose glare can turn other living things to stone.*

thiopia produces lynxes in great numbers, and sphinxes with brown hair and a pair of udders on the breast, and many other monstrosities—winged horses armed with horns, called *pegasi*, hyenas like a cross between a dog and a wolf, that break everything with their teeth, swallow it at a gulp and masticate it in the belly; tailed monkeys with black heads, ass's hair and a voice unlike that of any other species of ape; Indian oxen with one and with three horns; the *leucrocota*, swiftest of wild beasts, about the size of an ass, with a stag's haunches, a lion's neck, tail and breast, badger's head, cloven hoof, mouth opening right back to the ears, and ridges of bone in place of rows of teeth—this animal is reported to imitate the voices of human beings. Among the same people is also found the animal called the yale, the size of a hippopotamus, with an elephant's tail, of a black or tawny colour, with the jaws of a boar and movable horns more than a cubit in length which in a fight are erected alternately, and presented to the attack or sloped backward in turn as policy directs. But its fiercest animals are forest bulls, larger than the bulls of the field, surpassing all in speed, of a tawny colour, with blue eyes, hair turned backward, mouth gaping open to the ears, along with mobile horns; the hide has the hardness of flint, rejecting every wound. They hunt all wild animals, but themselves can only be caught in pits, and when caught always die game. Ctesias writes that in the same country is born the creature that he calls the *mantichora*, which has a triple row of teeth meeting like the teeth of a comb, the face and ears of a human being, grey eyes, a blood-red colour, a lion's body, inflicting stings with its tail in the manner of a scorpion, with a voice like the sound of a pan-pipe blended with a trumpet, of great speed, with a special appetite for human flesh.

He says that in India there are also oxen with solid hoofs and one horn, and a wild animal named *axis*, with the hide of a fawn but with more spots and white ones, belonging to the ritual of Father Liber (the Orsacan Indians hunt monkeys that are a bright white all over the body); but that the fiercest animal is the unicorn, which in the rest of the body resembles a horse, but in the head a stag, in the feet an elephant, and in the tail a boar, and has a deep bellow, and a single black horn three feet long projecting from the middle of the forehead. They say that it is impossible to capture this animal alive.

In Western Ethiopia there is a spring, the Nigris, which most people have supposed to be the source of the Nile, as they try to prove by the arguments that we have stated. In its neighbourhood there is an animal called the *catoblepas*, in other respects of moderate size and inactive with the rest of its limbs, only with a very heavy head which it carries with difficulty—it is always hanging down to the ground; otherwise it is deadly to the human race, as all who see its eyes expire immediately.

Catoblepas.

The basilisk serpent also has the same power. It is a native of the province of Cyrenaica, not more than 12 inches long, and adorned with a bright white marking on the head like a sort of diadem. It routs all snakes with its hiss, and does not move its body forward in manifold coils like the other snakes but advancing with its middle raised high. It kills bushes not only by its touch but also by its breath, scorches up grass and bursts rocks. Its effect on other animals is disastrous; it is

Basilisk.

believed that once one was killed with a spear by a man on horseback and the infection rising through the spear killed not only the rider but also the horse. Yet to a creature so marvellous as this—indeed kings have often wished to see a specimen when safely dead—the venom of weasels is fatal: so fixed is the decree of nature that nothing shall be without its match. They throw the basilisks into weasels' holes, which are easily known by the foulness of the ground, and the weasels kill them by their stench and die themselves at the same time, and nature's battle is accomplished.

From *Natural History*, Volume III, by Pliny the Elder. Translated by H. Rackham, Cambridge, Mass.: Harvard University Press, 1983, pp. 53-59.

The Griffin's Song

Barbara Wersba

In Barbara Wersba's Land of Forgotten Beasts *(1964), Andrew Peterson Smith is a scientific-minded modern boy who does not believe in the unbelievable. While looking at the* Book of Beasts *in a library one day, he fantastically enters the book he is reading, where he meets forgotten beasts of the imagination. At the climactic banquet of fabulous animals, the griffin sings—off-key—a song about his strange friends.*

The mushrush (sirrush) is a dragon-like Babylonian hybrid. Tree geese grow on trees like fruit (as their barnacle geese relatives hatch from barnacles). Half-horse and half-fish, the hippocampus is a literal sea horse. A two-headed serpent is the amphisbaena, with a head at each end of its body. A centaur is half-horse and half-man. Some sea creatures were thought to resemble monks and bishops. The ant-lion (myrmecoleon) has the face of a lion and the body of an ant.

h the world is filled with strangeness and delight.
There are fish that fly and birds that walk on land,
There are swans that sing and insects that do dances,
So why we're off I'll never understand.

We're courteous, unusual, and charming,
We're thoughtful and amazingly sincere.
We only need a little admiration
To fill our lives with happiness and cheer.

I will admit we're rather odd to look at,
Our heads and tails are sometimes out of place,
Occasionally we breathe a little fire,
But that should be no reason for disgrace.

The Cockatrice, for instance, is quite useful,
Though small, he has a mortifying glance.
If a mountain's in your way, he'll make it crumble,
His life is filled with danger and romance.

The Unicorn, by contrast, is so gentle
His horn can sweeten clouded pools and springs.
He lives on flowers and cannot be captured
By errant knights, or emperors, or kings.

The Manticore is equally appealing,
He jumps about and has a prickly tail.
Three rows of teeth and two superb mustaches,
You'll find him leaping over hill and dale.

Bishop fish.

Our country is incredibly exciting,
You'd never see a Mushrush back at home,
You couldn't grow a Goose Tree in Chicago,
You'd never find a Hippocamp in Rome.

Where else do serpents have two heads, or seven?
Where else are Centaurs quite so fancy-free?
Would you ever find a Griffin in your garden?
Do your Bishops ever frolic in the sea?

Your zoos are filled with simple things like Tigers,
Menageries like ours are more unique.
We have Ant-Lions, Phoenixes, and Dragons,
Our Mermaids are mysterious and chic.

We'll show you flying horses from the heavens,
We'll give you rides on monsters from the sea,
We'll take your hand and walk with you through fables,
Through legends filled with charm and poetry.

Though quite unreal, we're still the best beasts ever,
The fact that we're forgotten makes us weep.
The world that dreamed us cares for us no longer,
Its eyes are dim, its visions are asleep.

But some day Unicorns will be remembered,
And Griffins will again be brave and strong,
A Phoenix will be seen on the horizon
And all forgotten creatures shall belong.

From *The Land of Forgotten Beasts* by Barbara Wersba.
New York: Atheneum, 1964.

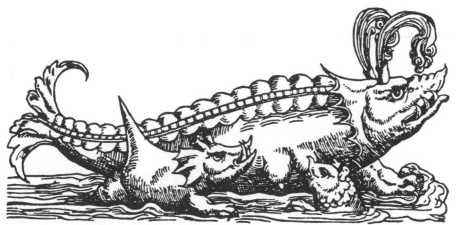

Sea monsters.

References

This hybrid list overlaps and supplements the entry sources listed in the acknowledgments. Included are both primary and secondary sources either cited or quoted in *Wonder Beasts*, used for background, consulted, or recommended for further reading.

Margaret Robinson's *Fictitious Beasts* is the only bibliography on the subject. Malcolm South's *Mythical and Fabulous Creatures: A Source Book and Research Guide*, a wealth of information and bibliographies, is the most comprehensive resource.

The modern classics that deal with either one or many of the wonder beasts are: Odell Shepard's *The Lore of the Unicorn*, T. H. White's *The Book of Beasts*, and Jorge Luis Borges's *The Book of Imaginary Beings*. Other major books on the subject include Peter Lum's *Fabulous Beasts* and Heinz Mode's *Fabulous Beasts and Demons*.

Aelian. *On the Characteristics of Animals*, Volume I. Translated by A. F. Scholfield. Cambridge, Mass.: Harvard University Press, 1971.

Allen, Judy, and Jeanne Griffiths. *The Book of the Dragon*. London: Orbis, 1979.

Allen, Richard Hinckley. *Star Names: Their Lore and Meaning*. G.E. Stechert, 1899. Reprint, New York: Dover Publications, 1963.

Almedingen, E. M. *Russian Folk and Fairy Tales*. New York: G. P. Putnam's Sons, 1957.

Arber, Edward, ed. *The First Three English Books in America*. Birmingham, England, 1885.

Barker, W. H., and Cecilia Sinclair. *West African Folk-Tales*. London: George G. Harrap, 1917.

Benjamin of Tudela. *The Itinerary of Benjamin of Tudela*. London, 1907. Reprint, New York: Philipp Feldheim, n.d.

Benton, Janetta Rebold. *The Medieval Menagerie: Animals in the Art of the Middle Ages*. New York: Abbeville Press, 1992.

Borges, Jorge Luis, with Margaritta Guerro. *The Book of Imaginary Beings*. Translated by Norman Thomas di Giovanni. New York: Avon Books, 1970.

Browne, Sir Thomas. *Pseudodoxia Epidemica (Vulgar Errors)*. London, 1646.

Budge, E. A. Wallis, trans. *The Egyptian Book of the Dead*. London, 1895. Reprint, New York: Dover Publications, 1969.

Burton, Richard F., ed. and trans. *The Thousand Nights and a Night*. Mecca Edition. n.d.

Carroll, Lewis. *Alice's Adventures in Wonderland*. Chicago: M. A. Donahue, 1904.

Church, Alfred John, and William Jackson Brodribb, trans. *The Annals of Tacitus*. London: Macmillan, 1877.

Clair, Colin. *Unnatural History: An Illustrated Bestiary*. New York: Abelard-Schuman, 1967.

The Complete Illustrated Stories of the Brothers Grimm. London, 1853; Reprint, Octopus Books, 1984.

Costello, Peter. *The Magic Zoo: The Natural History of Fabulous Animals*. New York: St. Martin's Press, 1979.

Curley, Michael J., ed. *Physiologus*. Austin: University of Texas Press, 1979.

Di Varthema, Ludovico (Lewis Vartoman). *The Travels of Ludovico Di Varthema*. Translated by John Winter Jones and edited by George Percy Badger. London: The Hakluyt Society, 1863.

Fairbairn, James. *Heraldic Crests: A Pictorial Archive of 4,424 Designs for Artists and Craftspeople*. New York: Dover Publications, 1993.

Finlay, Winifred. *Folk Tales from Moor and Mountain*. New York: Roy, 1969.

Firdausi. *The Shah Nameh*. Translated by James Atkinson. London: Frederick Warne, 1886.

Fox-Davies, A. C. *A Complete Guide to Heraldry*. London: Thomas Nelson and Sons, 1961.

Fox-Davies, Arthur Charles. *Heraldry: A Pictorial Archive for Artists & Designers*. New York: Dover Publications, 1991.

Gesner, Konrad. *Curious Woodcuts of Fanciful and Real Beasts*. New York: Dover Publications, 1971.

Giblin, James Cross. *The Truth About Unicorns*. New York: HarperCollins, 1991.

Goldsmid, Edmund. *Un-Natural History: or Myths of Ancient Science*. Edinburgh: Privately printed, 1886.

Gould, Charles. *Mythical Monsters*. London: W.H. Allen, 1886. Reprint, New York: Crescent Books, 1989.

Hathaway, Nancy. *The Unicorn*. New York: Viking, 1980.

Hargreaves, Joyce. *Hargreave's New Illustrated Bestiary*. Glastonbury, England: Gothic Image, 1990.

Henderson, William. *Folk-Lore of the Northern Counties of England and the Borders*. Norwich, England: The Folklore Society, 1866.

Hoch, Edward D. "The Last Unicorns." From *100 Great Fantasy Short Short Stories*. Edited by Isaac Asimov, Terry Carr, and Martin H. Greenberg. Garden City, N.Y.: Doubleday, 1984.

Hoult, Janet. *Dragons: Their History & Symbolism*. Glastonbury, England: Gothic Image, 1987.

Huber, Richard. *Treasury of Fantastic and Mythological Creatures*. New York: Dover Publications, 1981.

Huxley, Francis. *The Dragon: Nature of the Spirit, Spirit of Nature*. New York: Thames and Hudson, 1992.

Johnson, Henry Lewis. *Decorative Ornaments and Alphabets of the Renaissance*. New York: Dover Publications, 1991.

Kandel, Michael, ed. *The Cosmic Carnival of Stanislaw Lem: An Anthology of Entertaining Stories by the Modern Master of Science Fiction*. New York: Continuum, 1981.

Legge, James, trans. *The Sacred Books of China*. From The Sacred Books of the East series, F. Max Müller, ed. Oxford, England: Clarendon Press, 1879.

Ley, Willy. *Dawn of Zoology*. Englewood Ciffs, New Jersey: Prentice-Hall, 1968.

——. *Willy Ley's Exotic Zoology*. New York: Viking, 1959.

Lum, Peter. *Fabulous Beasts*. New York: Pantheon Books, 1951.

——. *Italian Fairy Tales*. Chicago: Follett, 1963.

Mackenzie, Donald A. *Myths and Legends of China and Japan*. Reprint, London: Bracken Books, 1992.

Mandeville, Sir John. *The Travels of Sir John Mandeville*. New York: Macmillan, 1905.

McCrindle, J. W., trans. *Ancient India: As Described by Ktêsias the Knidian*. Delhi, India: Manohar Reprints, 1973.

McHargue, Georgess. *The Beasts of Never*. Indianapolis: Bobbs-Merrill, 1968.

Mode, Heinz. *Fabulous Beasts and Demons*. Translated by Fabeltiere and Damonen. London: Phaidon, 1975.

Nesbit, E. *The Phoenix and the Carpet*. Reprint, London: Octopus Books, 1979.

Nigg, Joe. *The Book of Gryphons*. Cambridge, Mass.: Apple-wood Books, 1982.

——. *A Guide to the Imaginary Birds of the World*. Cambridge, Mass.: Apple-wood Books, 1984.

Ormondroyd, Edward. *David and the Phoenix*. Chicago: Follett, 1958.

Ovid (Publius Ovidius Naso). *The Metamorphoses*. Translated by Horace Gregory. New York: Viking, 1958.

Paré, Ambroise. *Of Poisons*. Translated by Thomas Johnson. London, 1634. Reprint, New York: Milford House, 1968.

Pelton, Mary Helen, and Jacqueline DiGennaro. *Images of a People: Tlingit Myths and Legends*. Englewood, Colo.: Libraries Unlimited, 1992.

Phillips, Ellen, ed. *Magical Beasts*. Alexandria, Va.: Time-Life Books, 1986.

Philostratus. *The Life of Apollonius of Tyana*. Translated by F. C. Conybeare. Cambridge, Mass.: Harvard University Press, 1960.

Pliny the Elder. *Natural History*, Volume III. Translated by H. Rackham. Cambridge, Mass.: Harvard University Press, 1983.

Polo, Marco. *The Travels of Marco Polo*. Translated by Sir Henry Yule and edited by Henri Cordier. London: John Murray, 1903. Reprint, New York: Dover Books, 1993.

Rawlinson, George, trans. *The History of Herodotus*. New York: D. Appleton, 1859.

Reade, W. Winwood. *Savage Africa*. New York: Harper and Brothers, 1864.

Robinson, Margaret W. *Fictitious Beasts; A Bibliography*. London: The Library Association, 1961.

Ross, Alexander. *Arcana Microcosmi*. London, 1652.

Shepard, Odell. *Lore of the Unicorn*. London, 1930. Reprint, New York: Avenel Books, 1982.

Silverberg, Barbara, ed. *Phoenix Feathers: A Collection of Mythical Monsters*. New York: Dutton, 1973.

Silverberg, Robert. *The Realm of Prester John*. Garden City, New York: Doubleday, 1972.

Smith, G. Elliot. *The Evolution of the Dragon*. 1919. Watchung, N.J.: Albert Saifer, 1990. Reprint.

South, Malcolm, ed. *Mythical and Fabulous Creatures: A Sourcebook and Research Guide*. Westport, Conn.: Greenwood Press, 1987. Reprint, New York: Peter Bedrick Books, 1988.

Steele, Robert, ed. *Mediaeval Lore from Bartholomew Anglicus*. London: E. Stock, 1893. Reprint, New York: Cooper Square, 1966.

Stockton, Frank. *The Griffin and the Minor Canon*. New York: Holt, Rinehart & Winston, 1963.

Topsell, Edward. *The Historie of Foure-Footed Beasts*. London, 1658. Reprint, Ann Arbor, Mich.: University Microfilms, 1962.

The Travels of Sir John Mandeville. New York: The Macmillan Company, 1905.

Tripp, Jr., Raymond P., editor and translator. *Beowulf, An Edition and Literary Translation, In Progress*. Denver, Colo.: The Society for New Language Study, 1990.

_____. *The Old English Phoenix*. Denver, Colo.: The Society for New Language Study, 1994.

Vinycomb, John. *Fictitious and Symbolic Creatures in Art*. London: Chapman and Hall, 1906.

Wendt, Herbert. *Out of Noah's Ark*. Boston: Houghton Mifflin, 1959.

Wersba, Barbara. *The Land of Forgotten Beasts*. Illustrated by Margot Tomes. New York: Atheneum, 1964.

White, T. H., ed. and trans. *The Book of Beasts*. New York: G.P. Putnam's Sons, 1954.

Whitfield, Peter. *The Image of the World: 20 Centuries of World Maps*. San Francisco: Pomegranate Books in association with the British Library, 1994.

Williams, C. A. S. *Outlines of Chinese Symbolism and Art Motives*. Rutland, Vermont: Charles E. Tuttle, 1976.

Wyndham, Robert. *Tales the People Tell in China*. New York: Julian Messner, 1971.

Index

Page numbers of illustrations are italicized.

About the Author

Wondering about a hybrid animal figure on an antique lamp led writer **Joe Nigg** to years of researching fabulous animals. Among his published books are the award-winning *Book of Gryphons* and *A Guide to the Imaginary Birds of the World*. His stories and articles have appeared in many publications, including *Cricket* and *Short Story International*. A graduate of the Iowa Writers' Workshop and Denver University's Writing Program, Dr. Nigg has taught at the high school and college levels and has shared his knowledge of mythical creatures with all ages, from preschoolers to seniors. He lives in Denver, where he makes his living as a writer and editor. Under the gaze of his study lamp's lion of the sea, he is now working on another book of fabulous beasts.